The
Quotable
Writer

Also in the *Quotable* Series:

The Quotable Executive by John Woods
The Quotable Historian by Alan Axelrod
The Quotable Woman by Carol Turkington

Other Books by William A. Gordon:

Four Dead in Ohio: Was There a Conspiracy at Kent State?
The Ultimate Hollywood Tour Book
*Shot on This Site: A Traveler's Guide to the Places and Locations
Used to Film Famous Movies and Television Shows*

The Quotable Writer

Words of Wisdom from Mark Twain, Aristotle, Oscar Wilde, Robert Frost, Erica Jong, and More

WILLIAM A. GORDON

McGraw-Hill

New York San Francisco Washington, D.C. Auckland Bogotá
Caracas Lisbon London Madrid Mexico City Milan
Montreal New Delhi San Juan Singapore
Sydney Tokyo Toronto

Library of Congress Cataloging-in-Publication Data

The quotable writer / [selected by] William A. Gordon.
   p. cm.
  Includes index.
  ISBN 0-07-135576-6
  1. Authorship—Quotations, maxims, etc. 2. Creative writing—
Quotations, maxims, etc. 3. Authors and publishers—Quotations,
maxims, etc. 4. Publishers and publishing—Quotations, maxims, etc.
I. Gordon, William A. II. Title.

PN171.Q6 Q68   2000
808'.02—dc21

99-047303

McGraw-Hill

A Division of The **McGraw·Hill** *Companies*

2 3 4 5 6 7 8 9 0 DOC/DOC 0 9 8 7 6 5 4 3 2 1 0

ISBN 0-07-135576-6

This book was set in Berkeley by North Market Street Graphics.
Printed and bound by R. R. Donnelley & Sons Company.

McGraw-Hill books are available at special quantity discounts to use as
premiums and sales promotions, or for use in corporate training programs.
For more information, please write to the Director of Special Sales,
Professional Publishing, McGraw-Hill, Two Penn Plaza, New York, NY
10121-2298. Or contact your local bookstore.

This book is printed on recycled, acid-free paper containing a
minimum of 50% recycled, de-inked fiber.

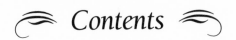

Contents

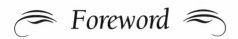

Foreword

"The perfect quote is to a writer as a flint is to a flame." If no one famous ever said that—and, as far as I know, no one has—someone should have. Because it's true: Finding the right quotation can spark an article, an essay, a story, a whole book. Some quotations have been such prolific story-starters, in fact, that they've degenerated into cliches. Not long ago, for example, the readers of *Writer's Digest's* e-mail newsletter demanded a moratorium on opening stories with a reference to F. Scott Fitzgerald's line about the rich being different. (Yeah, yeah, we know—they have more money.)

Is it any wonder, then, that writers vie with libraries as the most voracious consumers of collections of quotations? For most writers, good old *Bartlett's* is only the beginning of a lifelong, bookshelf-burdening quest for the perfect quotation.

Since writers love talking, thinking, and reading about writing and the literary life even more than they actually like writing (it's much easier, less stressful, and less likely to lead to carpal-tunnel syndrome), a collection of quotations *about* writing comes close to nirvana. If such a book can actually offer inspiration and instruction—words of wisdom from writers who've been there and done that—well, that brings us to *The Quotable Writer.*

William A. Gordon has created a *Bartlett's* of the literary life, culling and collecting roughly a thousand of the best things ever said or written by and about writers and writing. These are the kinds of quotes you'll want to enlarge and stick on your bulletin board or tape to the top of your computer monitor, to glance at for affirmation and encouragement when the blank page before you stubbornly stays blank. These are the words of wisdom from writers who've beaten writer's block, defeated deadlines, triumphed over transitions, and created characters for the ages. You'll hear, too, from writers who crashed and burned out in the literary life, and you'll realize that maybe your own writing woes aren't so bad, after all.

Can a single quotation—or even a book of a thousand quotations—change a life, jump-start a career, help you breakthrough to a byline, light a flame? Powerful words have done far more throughout history, from sparking revolutions (think Patrick Henry) to launching religions (think Jesus or Buddha). Writers, of all people, should appreciate the power of words.

The Quotable Writer taps the power of words for the wordsmiths who live and make their living by them. Dip into it and see if you don't find yourself driven to write some yourself.

David A. Fryxell
Editorial Director and Nonfiction Columnist
Writer's Digest

⌒ *Introduction* ⌒

The wisdom of the wise and the experience of the ages are perpetuated by quotations.

— Isaac Disraeli, *Curiosities of Literature*

This is an unusual type of quote book in that it is not just a reference tool that writers in need of a quote can turn to and come up with something memorable. This is also a book with a mission, and that mission is to help writers—whether they are just starting out or have already been published—by providing all kinds of practical advice about the craft of writing and the business of publishing.

In fact, this is a book I wish someone had given me when I started work on my first book some 25 years ago. Like so many authors, I did not ask the question: Who will buy this book, and why? I paid little attention to the marketplace and was basically ignorant of how the publishing business operates.

That, of course, helps explain why 17 years passed between the time I started working on my first book and the time it was eventually published. Since then I have written two other books, and can count myself among the fortunate few who are able to make a living as a full-time writer.

During the years I wandered around the publishing wilderness, I started collecting the quotes that appear in this volume, selecting them from various books, magazine and newspaper articles, and other sources. The quotes helped keep me sane, motivated, and focused.

I continued to collect quotes even after my first book was published, although not just any quotes. I only picked those quotes about writing and publishing that count and that struck me as being the most memorable, thought-provoking, humorous, and/or important.

This collection, which consists of approximately 1000 quotes, can almost be viewed as a Publishing 101 for those new to the business. It is my hope that it will also prove to be useful to others who work with the written word, including historians, journalists, speechwriters, English teachers, and screenwriters.

William A. Gordon

# Acknowledgments

For research assistance, I would like to thank Sarah Heller of the Authors Guild; Judith Krug of the American Library Association's Office of Intellectual Freedom and her staff; Jonathan R. Cole, director of the Center for Social Studies at Columbia University; Roger Rosenblatt of *Time* magazine; the late historian Page Smith; Professor Greg Johnson of Kennesaw State University; Dan Poynter, author of *The Self-Publishing Manual*; Paul Iacono of R. R. Bowker; Philip Bookman of the *Stockton Record*; Anne Tyler; the staffs of the American Council of Learned Societies, the American Historical Association, the Writers Guild of America West, and the Samuel Johnson Sound Bite Page; Pam Henstell, Lotchen Shivers, Amy Corley, and other publicists too numerous to mention; and the librarians at the University of Akron, the Akron-Summit County Library, the Orange County Public Library, the Newport Beach Public Library, and UCLA.

I would especially like to thank Paul Keane for his astute editorial suggestions; Nicholas T. Smith, my literary agent; and Nancy Mikhail, my editor at McGraw-Hill.

Grateful acknowledgment is made to the following for permission to reprint previously published material:

Harper & Row: Excerpts from *How to Get Happily Published: A Complete and Candid Guide* by Judith Appelbaum and Nancy Evans, copyright © 1978 by Judith Appelbaum and Nancy Evans.

Harper's magazine: Various quotations, copyright © 1981 and 1985 by *Harper's* magazine. All rights reserved. Reprinted by permission.

The Nation: Reprinted with permission from the October 3, 1981, November 20, 1982, March 24, 1984, May 27, 1996, June 3, 1996, and December 23, 1997 issues of *The Nation* magazine. Portions of each week's *The Nation* magazine can be accessed at http://www.thenation.com.

Paris Review: Various quotations, copyright © 1954–1981. Reprinted by permission.

Publishers Weekly: Various quotations, copyright © 1973–1998. Reprinted by permission.

Washington Post: Various quotations, copyright © 1983, 1984, 1997, and 1998. Reprinted by permission.

Every effort has been made to credit the original author, to secure every necessary permission, and to make full and just acknowledgment of sources; if we have failed in any case and if your favorite quote in any department does not appear, we ask for mercy and understanding and offer correction in another and enlarged edition.

—FRANK S. MEAD, editor, *The Encyclopedia of Religious Quotations*

The
Quotable
Writer

Biography

Every great man nowadays has his disciples and it is always Judas who writes the biography.
— OSCAR WILDE, *The Critic As Artist,* 1891

One of the new terrors of death.
— JOHN ARBUTHNOT, British writer, quoted in *The Poetical Works of Alexander Pope* edited by Robert Carruthers, 1858

Biography, like big game hunting, is one of the recognized forms of sport, and it is unfair as only sport can be.
— PHILIP GUEDALLA, *Supers and Supermen,* 1920

Biography is all about cutting people down to size.
— Attributed to ALAN BENNETT, British playwright

Pathography
— Term coined by JOYCE CAROL OATES, novelist, to describe sensational (or "drive-by") biographies whose "motifs are dysfunction and disaster, illnesses and pratfalls, failed marriages and failed careers, alcoholism and breakdowns and outrageous conduct," *The New York Times Book Review,* August 28, 1988

Nobody can write the life of a man but those who have eat and drunk and lived in social intercourse with him.
— SAMUEL JOHNSON, English writer, lexicographer, and critic, quoted in *Life of Johnson* by James Boswell, 1791

What a wee part of a person's life are his acts and his words! His real life is led in his head, and it is known to none but himself.
— MARK TWAIN, *Autobiography,* 1924

Autobiography is probably the most respectable form of lying.
— HUMPHREY CARPENTER, "Patrick White Explains Himself," *The New York Times Book Review,* February 7, 1982

What are the biographer's tools? Primary among them are sensitivity, common sense, compassion and a passion for the truth—the other academic things are easy to learn. I'm always surprised if someone remarks that my biographies of men and women deal so deeply with the subject's inner life. What other kind of life is there, I'd like to know? If the biographer doesn't give you the subject's inner life, all you're left with is an almanac entry.

> — DONALD SPOTO, author of biographies of Alfred Hitchcock, Tennessee Williams, Laurence Olivier, Marilyn Monroe, Jesus, and others, in an e-mail to William A. Gordon, July 14, 1998

To write one's memoirs is to speak ill of everybody except oneself.

> — HENRI PHILLIPE PETAIN, French military leader and statesman, quoted in *The Observer,* May 26, 1946

Biography is a noble and adventurous art, as noble as the making of painted portraits, poems, statues.

> — LEON EDEL, *Writing Lives,* 1984

Not all artists or historians have such an exalted notion of biography. Some feel it to be a prying, peeping and even predatory process.

> — LEON EDEL, *Writing Lives,* 1984

The biographer, indeed, is like the professional burglar, breaking into a house, rifling through certain drawers . . . The voyeurism and busybodyism that impel writers and readers of biography alike are obscured by an apparatus of scholarship designed to give the enterprise an appearance of banklike blandless and solidity.

> — JANET MALCOLM, *The Silent Woman: Sylvia Plath and Ted Hughes,* 1994

I wouldn't want the whole truth about me told. I don't feel I'm so perfect that I would like it recorded.

> — LADY ANTONIA FRASER, biographer, when *Time* magazine turned the tables on her and asked if she would like to be the subject of a biography written by another author, quoted in *Time,* July 13, 1998

The facts of a person's life, like murder, will come out.

> ━ NORMAN SHERRY, British educator, quoted in *International Herald Tribune*, September 15, 1989

[Biographers are] artists under oath.

> ━ DESMOND MCCARTHY, biographer, quoted in *Writing Lives* by Leon Edel, 1984

Blurbs

When a book comes into print today, suddenly there are ten false witnesses to testify it is the greatest which has ever appeared.

> ━ ISAAC BASHEVIS SINGER, short-story writer and novelist, quoted in *The Atlantic Monthly*, July 1970

Never underestimate the power of the blurb. It'll be read by more people than the book.

> ━ ALICE KAHN, "How to Judge a Book by Its Blurb," *Los Angeles Times*, January 13, 1991

An effective blurb . . . will generally be used again in promotional pieces, advertising, [and] sell copy—and believe it or not—in review columns describing the book.

> ━ STANLEY J. CORWIN, *How to Become a Bestselling Author*, 1984

Outside of the major metropolitan areas, reviewers tend to rewrite jacket copy [which sometimes include blurbs] or the publisher's press release.

> ━ JOHN GREGORY DUNNE, *Esquire*, February 1987

Cross-blurbers.

> ━ Term coined by *Vanity Fair* contributor HOWARD KAPLAN, who exposed authors who traded favorable blurbs with each other

Flap copy . . . serves as a crutch for lazy reviewers; good flap copy will be repeated in "review" after "review" around the country.

> — HUGH RAWSON, "The Editor's Role in Marketing," *Trade Book Marketing: A Practical Guide* edited by Robert A. Carter, 1983

Countless hours of editorial aggravation are spent ensuring that even the most lackluster volume can shine by reflected light.

> — CURT SUPLEE, reporter, *Washington Post*, January 5, 1982

The theory is that if a famous author says another author is terrific, the public, sheeplike, will line up and buy the book in question.

> — WILLIAM COLE, anthologist/publicist, *The New York Times Book Review*, July 23, 1978

I've worked in bookstores and have done a lot of selling and I've never seen anyone read blurbs. The customers don't care . . . I also think it's just friends helping friends.

> — KAY SEXTON, former director of merchandise communications, B. Dalton, quoted in *The Writing Business: A Poets & Writers Handbook*, 1985

The only thing blurbs actually prove is that the author has famous friends who owe him a favor.

> — CYNTHIA CROSSEN, publishing correspondent, *The Wall Street Journal*, July 14, 1988

The solicitation of advance blurbs for new books [is] a corrupt practice . . . that has grown wildly out of control.

> — CAMILLE PAGLIA, "The Unbridled Lust for Blurbs," *Publishers Weekly*, June 3, 1996

Any person furnishing a blurb for a book jacket . . . [should] be required to disclose his connections to the author of the book.

> — CALVIN TRILLIN, facetiously proposing an "open blurb law" to stop the misuse of blurbs, *Uncivil Liberties*, 1982

(For additional related quotes, see also *Publicity and Marketing*)

 *Books*

All books are divisible into two classes, the books of the hour and the books of all time.

— JOHN RUSKIN, *Sesame and Lilies*, 1865

All that mankind has done, thought or been: it is lying as in magic preservation in the pages of books.

— THOMAS CARLYLE, *On Heroes, Hero-Worship and the Heroic in History*, 1840

Whether for information, argument or entertainment, the book is considered a repository. One expects that the contents of a book will be available beyond the immediate moment—for years or generations into the future.

— LEONARD SHATZKIN, *In Cold Type*, 1982

Books still offer the most complete kind of understanding, and they last.

— Attributed to BOB WOODWARD, author and *Washington Post* reporter

Books are the main source of our knowledge, our reservoir of faith, memory, wisdom, morality, poetry, philosophy, history and science.

— DANIEL J. BOORSTIN, librarian of Congress, report, "Books in Our Future," 1984

Books through the ages have earned humanity's high regard as semi-sacred objects.

— RICHARD KLUGER, "The Cost of Integrity," *The Nation*, June 3, 1978

Books are the carriers of civilization.

— BARBARA TUCHMAN, historian, "The Book," lecture at the Library of Congress, October 17, 1979

Indeed, should civilization itself become extinguished, books will stand as its likeliest memorial.

➤ ROSALIE HEACOCK, literary agent, quoted in *Publishers Weekly,* January 25, 1985

If books were to disappear, history would disappear; so would men.

➤ JORGE LUIS BORGES, novelist, quoted in *Publishing Books* edited by Everette E. Dennis, Craig L. LaMay, and Edward C. Pease, 1997

Books are weapons in the war of ideas.

➤ Motto of the Council on Books in Wartime

Even bad books are books and therefore sacred.

➤ GUNTHER GRASS, *The Tin Drum,* 1964

Books, from Harriet Beecher Stowe's *Uncle Tom's Cabin,* through Upton Sinclair's *The Jungle* to Ralph Nader's *Unsafe at Any Speed* and Rachel Carson's *Silent Spring* in our own time have made a real difference in the way our society works and in how some of our corporations operate. There is still, even in this age of instant electronic communication and mass-circulation national magazines, something uniquely authoritative about a book.

➤ JOHN F. BAKER, *Publishers Weekly,* September 5, 1986

Certain books have exerted a profound influence on history, culture, civilization and scientific thought throughout recorded time . . . In every historical era, we find overwhelming evidence of the power of the written word, without which a high state of civilization and culture is inconceivable in any time or place.

➤ ROBERT B. DOWNS, *Books That Changed the World,* 1956

Clearly, books can be forces for both good and bad . . . Books are dynamic and powerful instruments, tools and weapons.

➤ ROBERT B. DOWNS, *Books That Changed the World,* 1956

Books are items of commerce offered for sale in public places. They are not sacred texts brought down from the mountains by gods and heroes.

➥ CLARKSON N. POTTER, *Who Does What and Why in Book Publishing*, 1990

More than ever, alas, a new book is not merely a joy, but a luxury.

➥ JONATHAN YARDLEY, **commenting on the rising cost of books,** *Washington Post*, **September 26, 1983**

 *Censorship*

The wonderful thing about libraries and bookstores—even the television or the radio—is that no one is forcing you to read anything, or to go to any particular movie, or to watch something on television or listen to something on the radio. You have free choice.

➥ JUDITH KRUG, **director, Office of Intellectual Freedom, American Library Association, interview with William A. Gordon, 1982**

Oh, sure. That is what the First Amendment is all about.

➥ JUDITH KRUG, **director, Office of Intellectual Freedom, American Library Association, answering a question if she would support the right to read a book advocating the overthrow of the U.S. government**

The trouble with censorship is that once it starts it is hard to stop. Just about every book contains something that someone objects to.

➥ STUDS TERKEL, **author and oral historian, quoted in** *U.S. News & World Report*, **March 8, 1982**

What is freedom of expression? Without the freedom to offend, it ceases to exist.

➥ SALMAN RUSHDIE, **Indian novelist, quoted in** *Weekend Guardian*, **February 10, 1990**

Literature should not be suppressed merely because it offends the moral code of the censor.

— WILLIAM O. DOUGLAS, U.S. Supreme Court Justice, in Dissent, *Roth v. U.S.,* 1957 Supreme Court decision

The point is that any sort of censorship is extremely dangerous. Nobody is wise enough to be a censor.

— MAXWELL E. PERKINS, editor, in a letter to an unidentified writer, May 29, 1947, quoted in *Editor to Author: The Letters to Maxwell E. Perkins* selected and edited by John Hall Wheelock, 1950

We can never be sure that the opinion we are endeavoring to stifle is a false opinion; and even if we are sure, stifling it would be an evil still.

— JOHN STUART MILL, *On Liberty,* 1859

They condemn what they do not understand.

— MARCUS FABIUS QUINTILIANUS, Roman rhetorician, *Quintilian's Institutes of Oratory, or, Education of an Orator,* 1895

It is impossible for ideas to compete in the marketplace if no forum for their presentation is provided or available.

— THOMAS MANN, German novelist, quoted in the American Library Association's *1996 Banned Books Resource Guide* by Robert Doyle

Whenever they burn books they will also, in the end, burn human beings.

— HEINRICH HEINE, *Almansor: A Tragedy,* 1823

The burning of an author's books, imprisonment for opinion's sake, has always been the tribute that an ignorant age pays to the genius of its time.

— JOSEPH LEWIS, *Voltaire: The Incomparable Infidel,* 1929

The books that the world calls immoral are books that show the world its shame.

— OSCAR WILDE, *The Picture of Dorian Gray,* 1891

There is no such thing as a moral or an immoral book. Books are well written, or badly written. That is all.

　— Oscar Wilde, Preface to *The Picture of Dorian Gray,* 1891

We have sold between 30,000 and 40,000 copies. Not enough to get spectacularly rich off of, but enough for us to keep them in print . . . Who is to determine that we can't publish these books? In our society, no one can ban the publication of these books, and that's as it should be.

　— Peter Lund, chairman, Paladin Press, and publisher of a five-volume series, *How to Kill,* quoted in *The New York Times,* July 1, 1981

Publishers have no unique right to abet murder.

　— Howard Siegel, lawyer, Rockville, Maryland, who successfully sued Paladin Press, publisher of *Hit Man,* a how-to-murder manual, after the book was found in the home of a contract killer who followed the book's instructions, quoted in *Publishers Weekly,* May 31, 1999

The way to kill germs and maggots is to bring them into the open, where they are recognized for what they are. It is when they are allowed to propagate under stones and in darkness that they grow strong and more harmful.

　— Maxwell E. Perkins, editor, in a letter to an unidentified writer, May 29, 1947, quoted in *Editor to Author: The Letters of Maxwell E. Perkins* selected and edited by John Hall Wheelock, 1950

Censorship always defeats its own purpose, for it creates in the end the kind of society that is incapable of exercising real discretion.

　— Henry Steele Commager, *Freedom, Loyalty and Dissent,* 1954

Censorship often begins at the threshold of good intentions. It is perhaps for that reason that I've found its grip so tenacious, that while it assumes new forms and shapes, it never quite disappears.

　— Martin Garbus, *Tough Talk: How I Fought for Writers, Comics, Bigots, and the American Way,* 1998

There's nothing that can stimulate interest in a book as quickly as when somebody tries to ban it.

➤ MIKE ROYKO, columnist, *Chicago Sun-Times*, February 13, 1981

That will sell 25,000 books for sure!

➤ MARK TWAIN, reaction to the Concord, Massachusetts, library's banning of *Huckleberry Finn,* in a 1885 letter to Charles L. Webster, his nephew and head of his publishing company, quoted in *Mark My Words* by Mark Dawidziak, 1996

Dear Mr. and Mrs. Younis:

I wish you great success in banning the book *Boss* from your local high school. And I offer my support.

It is a filthy sex perverted book, filled with shocking language and scenes too horrible to mention. Why, it would probably make Harold Robbins blush.

I hope that erotic, unspeakable book is banned before the birth-rate in your town soars.

By the way—I have another book on the market right now. If there's anything you can do about getting that one banned too, I'd really appreciate it.

➤ MIKE ROYKO, columnist, response to the attempts of a Hanibal, New York, couple that tried to ban his book *Boss. Chicago Sun-Times,* February 13, 1981

Making It With Mademoiselle

➤ The title of a book that was banned from a high school library. According to the American Library Association's Judith Krug, the censors thought it was pornographic; actually, it was a book about dressmaking patterns.

The Belly Button Defense

➤ Another banned title. This one, according to Krug, turned out to be about a basketball defense.

 *Classics*

[*Definition*] A classic is something that everybody wants to have read and nobody wants to read.

— MARK TWAIN, speech, "The Disappearance of Literature," 19th Century Club, November 20, 1900, quoted in *Mark Twain's Speeches* edited by Albert Bigelow Paine, 1923

 *Controversy*

Any authentic work of art must start an argument between the artist and his audience.

— REBECCA WEST, *The Court and the Castle,* 1957

If a book stirs up violent opposition and equally partisan feeling in support of its point of view, the probabilities are that it has deeply affected the thinking of people.

— ROBERT B. DOWNS, *Books That Changed the World,* 1956

It is advantageous to an author that his book should be attacked as well as praised. Fame is a shuttlecock. If it be struck at only one end of the room, it will soon fall to the ground. To keep it up, it must be struck at both ends.

— SAMUEL JOHNSON, **English writer, lexicographer, and critic,** quoted in *The Crown Treasury of Relevant Quotations* by Edward F. Murphy, 1978

You can be denounced from the heavens, and it only makes people interested.

— Attributed to TOM WOLFE, **journalist and novelist**

To brand a book with infamy is to insure its sale.

➣ JAMES RIDLEY, *The History of James Lovegrove,* 1761

If you are not sometimes attacked, then you cannot be very good . . . the attack itself is a certification of worth.

➣ JOHN GREGORY DUNNE, "Slings and Arrows," *Esquire,* February 1987

With the cost of book production ever on the rise, fewer risks can be taken; the quiet writer must defer to the shocking and outrageous.

➣ NONA BALAKIN, *Critical Encounters,* 1978

Artists are meant to be madmen, to disturb and shock us.

➣ ANNE RICE, novelist, quoted in the *Seattle Times,* December 13, 1990

We all live in a society where the more outrageous you are, the more publicity you get.

➣ ROGER SIMON, columnist, *Baltimore Sun,* October 1, 1985

Get them talking, even if it's all negative word of mouth. What do you care as long as they spell your name right?

➣ JOHN WATERS, filmmaker, *National Lampoon,* May 1985

When a thing ceases to be a subject of controversy, it ceases to be a subject of interest.

➣ WILLIAM HAZLITT, *Collected Works,* 1902

 *Creativity*

Something awful happens to a person who grows up as a creative kid and suddenly finds no creative outlet as an adult.

➣ JUDY BLUME, novelist, quoted in *Writer's Digest,* February 1979

I'm constantly amazed how creative a lot of people are who aren't in the creative fields. I sometimes think that we in the so-called arts think we have a lock on sensitivity and creativity. And hell, a guy comes to the house to paint a fence, and when you talk to him and watch him work, you suddenly realize that he, in his own way, is as creative and sensitive as anybody you're working with in the so-called arts.

━ NORMAN LEAR, producer, quoted in *How the Great Comedy Writers Create Laughter* by Larry Wilde, 1976

I'm not sure I understand the creative process. I've never given much attention to it. I understand how I work, but I really don't know what psychological things happen in the creative process, or why someone creates.

━ PADDY CHAYEFSKY, screenwriter, quoted in *The Craft of the Screenwriter* by John Brady, 1981

[*Definition*] It's the ability to see things in a new way, and from that insight to produce something that didn't exist before—something original.

━ BILL MOYERS, journalist, quoted in *The Writer*, April 1983

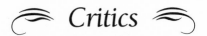 *Critics*

You're there to be shot at, and that's part of it.

━ Attributed to NORMAN MAILER, novelist

After something is published, all I want to read or hear is praise. Anything less is a bore.

━ TRUMAN CAPOTE, novelist, quoted in *The Paris Review*, Spring/Summer 1957

It's easier to write about those you hate—just as it's easier to criticize a bad play or a bad book.

➤ DOROTHY PARKER, critic, quoted in *The Paris Review,* Spring 1956

Some reviews give pain. This is regrettable, but no author has any right to whine. He is not obliged to be an author. He invited publicity, and he must take the publicity that comes along.

➤ E. M. FORSTER, English novelist and critic, essay in *The Author,* Summer 1943

Vigorous criticism stings, but I've learned that if the critic hadn't taken me seriously, he wouldn't have put so much energy into the mugging.

➤ JOHN LONG, *Writer's Little Book of Wisdom,* 1996

The important thing is that you make sure that neither the favorable nor the unfavorable critics move into your head and take part in the composition of your next work.

➤ THORNTON WILDER, playwright and novelist, quoted in *The Paris Review,* Winter 1957

There's only one person a writer should listen to, pay any attention to. It's not any damn critic. It's the reader.

➤ WILLIAM STYRON, novelist, quoted in *The Paris Review,* Spring 1954

The public is the only critic whose judgment is worth anything at all . . . Many wiser and better men than you poo-poohed Shakespeare, even as late as two centuries ago; but that old party has outlived these people.

➤ MARK TWAIN, *Autobiography,* 1924

A good writer is not, per se, a good book critic. No more so than a good drunk is automatically a good bartender.

➤ JIM BISHOP, *New York Journal-American,* November 26, 1957

It is not the critic who counts, nor the man who points out how the strong man stumbles, or where the doer of deeds could have done better. The credit belongs to the man who is actually in the arena.

— President THEODORE ROOSEVELT, quoted by President Richard Nixon in his resignation speech, August 8, 1974

If a writer is discouraged by critics, he shouldn't be a writer.

— DARRYL PONICSCAN, novelist, quoted in "*I Get My Best Ideas in Bed*": *And Other Words of Wisdom from 190 of America's Best-Selling Authors* edited by William Melton, 1971

Pay no attention to what the critics say; no statue has ever been put up to a critic.

— Attributed to JEAN SIBELIUS, Finnish composer, after an English critic called Sibelius's Seventh Symphony a failure

A book will be praised for many reasons. One review will praise a book for its optimism, another for its pessimism.

— ISAAC BASHEVIS SINGER, short-story writer and novelist, quoted in *The Atlantic Monthly*, July 1970

In literary criticism there are no criteria, no accepted standards of excellence by which to test the work.

— AMBROSE BIERCE, *The Collected Works of Ambrose Bierce*, Volume X, 1909

Good reviews do get written, but most book reviewing in this country is mediocre, and quite possibly always will be. The people who do reviewing do it as a bit of work peripheral to work that is more truly at the center of their lives.

— JOSEPH EPSTEIN, *Plausible Prejudices*, 1985

When a writer spends years of his life writing a book, you owe it to him to say, "With the best will in the world, I tried to read this and failed, and here's why," not sit on some judgment seat.

— NORMAN MAILER, novelist, quoted in *New York* magazine, February 3, 1986

As a reviewer, I've always tried to ask: "What did this author set out to do, and how well did he or she do it?" instead of "What do I think this author ought to have set out to do?"

➤ JANICE HARAYDA, book editor, Cleveland's *Plain Dealer*, July 19, 1987

The best literary critic is the one who understands what the author was unable, for one reason or another, to write; and understanding this, is able to more appreciatively evaluate what the author was able to achieve.

➤ PAUL HORGAN, *Approaches to Writing*, 1988

The most important function [of the critic] is to make known good things that are around so that people want to read them.

➤ MARY GORDON, novelist, quoted in *Commonweal*, May 9, 1980

I like to think of a new book as a mysterious geological treasure, a rock never before handled. The delighted discoverers' first, most natural response is, what have we here? I hold the rock in the palm of my hand to examine it: what are its colors, its contours, its special beauty (or ugliness)? Is it like others I've seen, enough like them, even to fit into a generic category? Is it more or less beautiful than those of its kind? Or is it, though it bears a surface family resemblance, distinguished by intriguing, individual markings?

➤ LYNNE SHARON SCHWARTZ, "Getting Started in Book Reviewing," *The Writer*, December 1980

A true critic ought to dwell upon excellencies [sic] rather than imperfections, to discover the concealed beauties of a writer, and communicate to the world such things as are worth their observation.

➤ JOSEPH ADDISON, English poet/playwright/essayist, *The Spectator*, No. 291, February 2, 1712

Critics are like eunuchs in a harem; they know how it's done, they've seen it done every day, but they're unable to do it themselves.

➤ Attributed to BRENDAN BEHAN, Irish playwright

Many critics are like woodpeckers who, instead of enjoying the fruit and shadow of a tree, hop incessantly around the trunk pecking holes in the bark to discover some little worm or other.

> ← HENRY WADSWORTH LONGFELLOW, poet, quoted in *The Literary Life and Other Curiosities* by Robert Hendrickson, 1981

A critic is a man who expects miracles.

> ← JAMES GIBBONS HUNEKER, *Iconoclasts*, 1905

A critic is a man who knows the way but can't drive the car.

> ← KENNETH TYNAN, *The New York Times Magazine*, January 9, 1966

You know who the critics are?—the men who have failed in literature and art.

> ← BENJAMIN DISRAELI, *Lothair*, 1870

He who would write and can't write can surely review.

> ← JAMES RUSSELL LOWELL, *A Fable for Critics*, 1848

Little old ladies of both sexes.

> ← JOHN O'HARA, novelist, quoted in *The New York Times Book Review*, January 6, 1985

Asking a working writer what he thinks about critics is like asking a lamppost what it feels about dogs.

> ← CHRISTOPHER HAMPTON, British playwright, quoted in the *Sun Times Magazine*, October 16, 1977

The most unrestrained attacks have usually been directed at writers who succeed in reaching an enormous audience.

> ← MYRICK LAND, *The Fine Art of Literary Mayhem*, 1983

The writer must cultivate his arrogance and have no regard for these parasites.

> ← RICHARD CONDON, novelist, quoted in *Conversations* by Roy Newquist, 1967

There are perhaps a hundred writers in America who make a living from writing fiction . . . You can count them, really, on just a few people's hands. This, by the way, accounts for the viciousness of the criticism that commercially successful writers receive. It accounts for it almost better than anything because the only word to explain it is "envy," really.

➤ ERICA JONG, novelist, quoted in *Interviews with Contemporary Novelists* by Diana Cooper-Clark, 1986

Authors must be the only craftsmen in the world who have to submit to the criticism of inexperienced or incompetent people. A surgeon is not obliged to listen to the complaints of a student walking the wards for the first time, nor is he subjected to the rebukes of men whose patients have perished under their knives.

➤ ST. JOHN ERVINE, Irish playwright and novelist, quoted in *The Author,* Summer 1943

I have long felt that any reviewer who expresses rage and loathing for a novel is preposterous. He or she is like a person who has put on full armor and attacked a hot fudge sundae or banana split.

➤ KURT VONNEGUT, novelist, quoted in *Rotten Reviews: A Literary Companion* edited by Bill Henderson, 1986

There are some books which cannot be adequately reviewed for twenty or thirty years after they come out.

➤ JOHN MORLEY, *Recollections,* 1917

When the critics come around it's always too late.

➤ SIR SIDNEY NOLAN, Australian artist, London *Daily Telegraph,* September 15, 1992

I have never kept count, but my guess is that I have had roughly three hundred reviews bestowed on books I have written. From these three hundred or so reviews I have learned nothing, either about my books or about my quality as a writer.

➤ JOSEPH EPSTEIN, *Plausible Prejudices,* 1985

There is only one thing worse than a bad review, being ignored altogether.

> ➤ THEODORE WHITE, historian, quoted in *The New York Times*, July 24, 1982

I would rather be attacked than unnoticed. For the worst thing you can do to an author is to be silent as to his works.

> ➤ SAMUEL JOHNSON, English writer, lexicographer, and critic, quoted in *Life of Johnson* by James Boswell, 1791

The only impeccable writers are those who never wrote.

> ➤ WILLIAM HAZLITT, English essayist, "On the Aristocracy of Letters," *Table Talk*, 1821–1822

To escape criticism, do nothing, say nothing, be nothing.

> ➤ ELBERT HUBBARD, *Epigrams*, 1923

Certainly America is not overrun by great literary critics. The way I feel about reviews—my career has really been made by them, because I have gotten mostly good reviews. I am always happy to get good reviews because I want people to buy my books. But by and large, with some exceptions, your good reviews are usually as stupid as your bad reviews.

> ➤ FRAN LEBOWITZ, humorist, interview with William A. Gordon, 1983

We've got 40,000 books published each year, and 90% of them are swill.

> ➤ JOHN LEONARD, former *New York Times* book editor and self-appointed "commissar of literary culture," remark on *First Edition*, 1984

Nothing is more painful to me than the disdain with which people treat second-rate authors, as if there were room only for first-raters.

> ➤ Attributed to CHARLES AUGUSTIN SAINT-BEUEVE, French writer/critic

In literature, as in love, we are astonished at what is chosen by others.

→ ANDRÉ MAUROIS, French biographer, quoted in *The New York Times,* April 14, 1963

Our junk never gets reviewed, theirs does.

→ Anonymous editor in chief of a publishing house, complaining that *The New York Times Book Review* showed favoritism to books published by Times Books (then owned by the *Times*), quoted in *Books: The Culture and Commerce of Publishing* by Lewis Coser, Charles Kadushin, and Walter W. Powell, 1982

I am sitting in the smallest room in my house. I have your review in front of me. Soon it will be behind me.

→ MAX REGER, German composer, quoted in *Lexicon of Musical Invective* by Nicolas Slonimsky, 1965

Can anything be done about a bad review that was manifestly unfair? No. Even if a protest is published as a letter in a later issue of the rag, no one reads it.

→ CLARKSON N. POTTER, *Who Does What and Why in Book Publishing,* 1990

[I] would never think of writing a rebuttal . . . Having the letter printed would only compound the felony.

→ FAYE MOSKOWITZ, short-story writer, quoted in *Poets & Writers* magazine, July/August 1990

Let the reviews die of their own poison. Once or twice I've written bitter and noxious replies, then hid them in a drawer, feeling too proud to show my pain to the public. Months later, when I came across them, the whole business seemed too insignificant to bother about.

→ LYNNE SHARON SCHWARTZ, novelist, quoted in *Poets & Writers* magazine, July/August 1990

The best thing you can do about critics is never say a word. In the end you have the last say, and they know it.

→ Attributed to TENNESSEE WILLIAMS, playwright

Remember that the reviewer who dismissed you with a sneer will, if the book is a success, greet you five years later with: "How much I did enjoy that book!"

— DORIS LESSING, English novelist, "Into the Labyrinth," essay in *Author! Author!* edited by Richard Findlater, 1984

The whole business [of reviewing] is complicated, perverse, and bears little relation to common sense, need, commerce or literature.

— JOSEPH EPSTEIN, *Plausible Prejudices,* 1985

On the basis of the information at hand, we cannot say whether the frequency with which authors' books are reviewed is related to their financial return, nor can we say whether good reviews count more than bad ones.

— PAUL WILLIAM KINGSTON and JONATHAN R. COLE, professors, "Economic and Social Aspects of the Literary Situation," *Public Opinion Quarterly* (The authors also concluded that "being reviewed has little relation to earning a respectable income.")

 *Editors*

An editor should have a pimp for a brother, so he'd have somebody to look up to.

— Remark by GENE FOWLER, former managing editor, *New York American,* recalled by his son Will Fowler in a letter to William A. Gordon, August 13, 1999

No passion on earth, neither love or hate, is equal to the passion to alter someone else's draft.

— H. G. WELLS, quoted in *How to Enjoy Writing* by Janet Isamov and Isaac Isamov, 1987

Editing is the same thing as quarreling with writers—same thing exactly.

> ⟶ HAROLD ROSS, editor of *The New Yorker,* quoted in *Time,* March 6, 1950

I cannot think of anybody who doesn't need an editor, even though some people claim they don't.

> ⟶ Attributed to TONI MORRISON, novelist and editor

Even Noble Laureates can benefit from the comments of a good editor.

> ⟶ COLLEEN MCCULLOUGH, novelist, quoted in *Writer's Digest,* August 1994

There is no one else an author can trust to be impartial and honest about his or her writing.

> ⟶ OLGA LITOWINSKY, editor, *Publishers Weekly,* April 5, 1985

They can cast new and different beams of light on your work, and highlight things that you haven't really thought of.

> ⟶ VICTOR KELLEHER, fantasy writer, quoted in *How Writers Write* by Pamela Lloyd, 1990

Writing is a two-person job. Even if you are a skilled editor of your own work, a second skilled editor will make suggestions you will inevitably miss, simply because, as the author, you lose a certain amount of objectivity.

> ⟶ SUSAN PAGE, *The Shortest Distance Between You and a Published Book,* 1997

By and large, the novels we buy are 95% ready for publication. We don't have the time to do much else with twenty-four or more books in production a year and reading on average two to three manuscripts a week, on top of all the line editing, conferences, and other work that has to be done.

> ⟶ PETER RUBIE, "An Editor Speaks From the Trenches," *The Writer,* September 1992

I see my role as helping the writer to realize his or her intention.

> ── FAITH SALE, vice president, G. P. Putnam's Sons, "Editing Fiction," *Editors on Editing* edited by Gerald Gross, 1962

My definition of a good editor is a man who I think charming, who sends me large checks, praises my work, my physical beauty, and my sexual prowess, and who has a stranglehold on the publisher and the bank.

> ── JOHN CHEEVER, novelist, quoted in *Writers at Work,* Fifth Series, 1981

Editors are extremely fallible people, all of them. Don't put too much trust in them.

> ── MAXWELL E. PERKINS, editor, quoted in *Max Perkins: Editor of Genius* by A. Scott Berg, 1978

By the nature of their profession they read too much, with the result that they grow jaded and cannot see talent when it dances in front of them.

> ── JOHN GARDNER, *On Becoming a Novelist,* 1983

Editors often made me think of giant grasshoppers, the way they hop from place to place. Fully aware of the fact that they are more poorly paid than most garbage collectors, they must be constantly on the watch for some new spot that offers a better deal.

> ── DONALD MACCAMPBELL, *The Writing Business,* 1978

If an editor lasts one year at a publishing house, I'm happy— honestly.

> ── JEAN NAGGAR, agent, explaining why she urges her clients to complete their books as soon as possible, quoted in *The Writing Business: A Poets & Writers Handbook,* 1985

Don't pass judgment on a manuscript as it is, but as it can be made to be.

> ── Advice to editors by Simon & Schuster founder M. LINCOLN SCHUSTER, quoted in *American Authors and the Literary Marketplace Since 1900* edited by James L. West, III, 1988

The most important friend a book has is the editor who acquired it . . . Because enthusiasm is the most important attitude in the publishing process, as long as that editor remains in place, you can expect a certain measure of commitment to see a book through, to ignite company enthusiasm, talk the book up to the trade, push the salespeople—and if nothing else, make the author feel that someone is watching over his or her baby . . . The departure of an editor is a traumatic event in the life of a book.

— RICHARD CURTIS, *This Business of Publishing,* 1998

It was not long ago that the prevailing attitude among editors was, "This book has some problems, but the author is so talented that I'd like to buy it and work with him." Today such words are rarely heard. A book with problems is a book rejected, and more and more one hears editors say, "Let the author revise, then we'll decide if we want to buy it."

— RICHARD CURTIS, literary agent, "Are Editors Necessary?" in *Editors on Editing,* third edition, edited by Gerald Gross, 1962

The manuscript you submit [should not] contain any flaws that you can identify—it is up to the writer to do the work, rather than counting on some stranger in Manhattan to do it for him.

— RICHARD NORTH PATTERSON, novelist, quoted in *Writer's Digest,* August 1994

(For additional related quotes, see also *Revision*)

 *Fame*

The best kind of fame is a writer's fame. Just enough to get a good table at a restaurant, and not enough for someone to interrupt you while you are eating.

— FRAN LEBOWITZ, humorist, quoted in *Us* magazine, August 1993

If you want a place in the sun, you've got to expect a few blisters.
— Anonymous

Footnotes

[*Definition*] Scholarly barbed-wire.
— EDMUND WILSON, literary critic, quoted in *Princeton Alumni Weekly*, December 4, 1973

Readers are like sheep. If there's any gate to the right or left, they'll take it. You must, therefore, always keep them on the path.
— PETER JACOBI, professor, Indiana University, quoted in *Writer's Digest*, August 1987

Don't use footnotes as a junkyard for all the words you cut from the text but couldn't bear to part with. Footnotes can be distracting, ugly, and they frequently work against you because the reader can't remember what he knows from the text and what he knows from the footnotes.
— GARY PROVOST, *100 Ways to Improve Your Writing*, 1985

Freelance Writers

[*Definition*] One who gets paid per word, per piece, or perhaps.
— ROBERT BENCHLEY, humorist, quoted in *Selected Letters of James Thurber* edited by H. Thurber and J. Weeks, 1981

 *Genius*

[*Definition*] A fellow who is a crackpot, until he hits the jacket.
▬ Unknown

[*Definition*] A man who is ahead of his time, but behind in his rent.
▬ Unknown

[*Definition*] One who offends his time, his country, his relatives.
▬ ELBERT HUBBARD, *A Thousand and One Epigrams*, 1923

[*Definition*] One who shoots at something no one else can see, and hits it.
▬ Unknown

Every man of genius sees the world at a different angle from his fellows.
▬ HAVELOCK ELLIS, *The Dance of Life*, 1923

True genius resides in the capacity for evaluation of uncertain, hazardous and conflicting information.
▬ Attributed to WINSTON CHURCHILL, British prime minister

It's no fun being a genius when you are the only one who knows about it.
▬ A writer who prefers to remain anonymous

It is impossible that a genius—at least a literary genius—can ever be discovered by his intimates; they are so close to him that he is out of focus to them . . . They can't get a perspective on him, and it is only by perspective that difference between him and the rest of their limited circle can be perceived.
▬ MARK TWAIN, quoted in *Mark Twain in Eruption* edited by Bernard DeVoto, 1940

Great geniuses have the shortest biographies. Their cousins can tell you nothing about them.

➤ RALPH WALDO EMERSON, *Representative Men,* 1850

The public is wonderfully tolerant. It forgives everything except genius.

➤ OSCAR WILDE, *The Critic As Artist,* 1891

Talent—genius, if you will—survives the most stringent oppression. Quality and distinction are in almost all cases recognized eventually. It's only a matter of luck and timing (but the timing, unfortunately, can be way off).

➤ WILLIAM MCPHERSON, *The Nation,* October 3, 1981

Genius, in fact, may be defined as the ability to control luck.

➤ Attributed to LANCE MORROW, *Time* essayist

There is no great genius without some touch of madness.

➤ **SENECA, Roman philosopher, quoting Greek philosopher Aristotle, "On Tranquility and the Mind," treatise in *Seneca's Moral Essays* edited by John F. Hurst and Henry Whiting, 1877**

I don't know who was the more appalled; my former teachers, who refused to believe it, or my family, who didn't want to believe it.

➤ **TRUMAN CAPOTE, novelist, describing reactions to the determination that his IQ was in the genius category, quoted in *The Paris Review,* Spring/Summer 1957**

Genius . . . [gets] its possessors into trouble of all kinds.

➤ **SAMUEL BUTLER, *Satires and Miscellaneous Poetry and Prose* edited by Rene Lamar, 1928**

A Confederacy of Dunces

➤ **Title of a tragicomic novel by JOHN KENNEDY TOOLE, who, according to his mother, committed suicide because he could not find a publisher. Twelve years after his death, the book won the 1980 Pulitzer Prize for fiction.**

In the republic of mediocrity, genius is dangerous.

➤ ROBERT G. INGERSOLL, lawyer, quoted in *Barnes & Noble Book of Quotations* edited by Robert I. Fitzhenry, 1983

The world has a standing pique against genius.

➤ WILLIAM HAZLITT, "On Genius and Common Sense," in *Table-Talk; or Original Essays by William Hazlitt*, 1821

When a true genius appears in the world, you may know him by this sign, that the dunces are all in confederacy against him.

➤ JONATHAN SWIFT, *Thoughts on Various Subjects*, 1706

Grammar

The rights of nations and kings sink into questions of grammar if grammarians discuss them.

➤ SAMUEL JOHNSON, English lexicographer, *Lives of the English Poets*, Volume 1, edited by George Birkbeck and Norman Hill, 1905

If all the grammarians in the world were placed end to end, it would be a good thing.

➤ Unknown

History, The Writing of

When it comes to the writing of history, few American historians, biographers and memorialists have made much of a mark.

➤ JAMES KILPATRICK, syndicated columnist, March 25, 1982

What makes a good writer of history is a guy who is suspicious. It marks the real differences between the man who wants to write honest history and the one who'd rather write a good story.

 ━ JAMES BISHOP, journalist, quoted in *The New York Times,*
    February 5, 1955

By whom is the real history being written today?—by whom has most of it been written in recent years? To an overwhelming extent, by the men and women furthest removed from the deadly touch of the academic glossologists . . . By far the larger number of our best historical writers are to be found outside academic lines.

 ━ ALLAN NEVINS, *Gateway to History,* 1962

Perhaps the academic historian suffers from having a captive audience, first in the supervisor of his dissertation, then in the lecture hall. Keeping the reader turning the page has not been his primary concern.

 ━ BARBARA TUCHMAN, *Practicing History,* 1981

When historians neglect the literary aspect of their discipline—and they forget that good history begins with a good story—they risk losing the wider audience that all great historians have addressed. They end up, sadly, talking to themselves.

 ━ JAMES WEST DAVIDSON and MARK HAMILTON LYTTLE, *After the Fact:*
    The Art of Historical Detection, 1982

History is not just scholarship. It is a branch of literature. The historian who presents information unadorned by art has done only half his job.

 ━ ORVILLE PRESCOTT, *History As Literature,* 1970

It is almost an insult to a historian . . . to say that his work can be recognized by its literary style. It is not his business to have a style.

 ━ H. MORSE STEPHENS, president, American Historical Society,
    1915, quoted in *Dissenting Opinions: Selected Essays* by Page
    Smith, 1984

What is the original research the professor must perform? Frequently it is a grubby little monograph on some obscure point that is of no general interest, written without skill or wit, published in a small, money-losing edition, to secure promotion.

— PAGE SMITH, *Dissenting Opinions: Selected Essays,* 1984

Academic prestige goes to those who can write in a dense style, difficult to understand, on a topic of little or no practical value.

— WILLIAM O'TOOLE, Cleveland's *Plain Dealer,* August 1, 1985

What good is their knowledge if it is merely to be passed around in a small circle of them?

— PAGE SMITH, historian, quoted in *Publishers Weekly,*
June 21, 1985

Is it not time that we scholars began to earn our keep in the world? Thanks to a gullible public, we have been honored, flattered, even paid, for producing the largest number of inconsequential studies in the history of civilization.

— HOWARD ZINN, *The Politics of History,* 1971

The history that lies inert in unread books does no work in the world.

— CARL BECKER, *American Historical Review,* January 1932

The purpose of history is not only to recover the past and to inform; it is also to stimulate thought, to delight, and to entertain.

— ORVILLE PRESCOTT, *History As Literature,* 1970

The historian must have some conception of how men who are not historians behave. Otherwise he will move in a world of the dead.

— E. M. FORSTER, *Abinger Harvest,* 1936

What historians sell is understanding.

— HAROLD PERKIN, *History: An Outline for the Intending Student,*
1970

When students and school boards ask Why history? What are we supposed to be getting out of this? the best answer is still that one word: judgment. We demand it of all professionals: doctors, lawyers, chefs and quarterbacks. And we need it most in the profession of citizenship, which, like it or not, exercise it or not, we are all born into.

➤ PAUL GAGNON, "Why Study History," *The Atlantic Monthly,* November 1988

People want to know about the past because they want to know how they came to be who they are, and how things came to be as they are . . . History—the study of the past—tells us how we got into the mess we are in.

➤ MILTON HIMMELFARB, *Commentary,* August 1970

Every one of the social sciences has its own contribution to make to the knowledge of man. The contribution of history is perspective.

➤ DAVID S. LANDES and CHARLES TILLEY, *History As a Social Science,* 1971

The value of history, then, is that it teaches us what man has done and thus what is.

➤ R. G. COLLINGWOOD, *The Idea of History,* 1946

History . . . helps people to learn something of themselves, perhaps in the way that a psychoanalyst seeks to help a patient.

➤ DAVID HACKETT FISCHER, *Historians' Fallacies,* 1970

History tells us who we are and how to behave.

➤ WILLIAM H. MCNEIL, *American History Illustrated,* March/April 1991

Actually, partisanship often adds zest for historical writing; for partisanship is an expression of interest and excitement and passion, and these can stir the reader as judiciousness might not.

➤ HENRY STEELE COMMAGER, *The Study of History,* 1956

We necessarily look to professional historians to help us sort out the differences between fact and fiction.

➤ ALLAN H. ROSENFELD, *Imagining Hitler*, 1985

The scholar is the guardian of memories . . . Where scholarship decays, myths will crowd in.

➤ E. H. GOMBRICH, art historian, *Meditations on a Hobby Horse*, 1963

God cannot alter the past, [but] historians can.

➤ SAMUEL BUTLER, *Prose Observations*, 1979

History is too serious to be left to the historians.

➤ IAIAN MACLEOD, *The Observer*, July 16, 1961

It requires an impartial man to make a good historian; but it is the partial and one-sided who hunt out the materials.

➤ Attributed to JOHN ACTON, English historian

The historian looks backward; eventually he also believes backward.

➤ FREIDERICH WILHELM NIETZSCHE, *The Twilight of the Idols*, 1888

History is always written wrong, and so always needs to be rewritten.

➤ GEORGE SANTAYANA, *The Life of Reason*, 1953

Although this work is History, I believe it to be true.

➤ MARK TWAIN, opening words, "3000 Years Among the Microbes," in *Mark Twain's Which Way Was That Dream? And Other Symbolic Writings of the Later Years* edited by John S. Tuckers, 1967

Historical events occur twice—the first time as tragedy, the second as farce.

➤ KARL MARX, *The Eighteenth Brumaire of Louis Bonaparte*, 1919

History is an argument without end.

➤ SIMON SCHAMA, historian, quoted in *Publishers Weekly*, May 17, 1991

The secret of historical composition is to know what to neglect.

▬ LORD BRYCE, *Studies in History and Jurisprudence,* 1901

The chief problem in historical honesty is not outright dishonesty. It is omission or deemphasis of important data. The definition of important, of course, depends on one's values.

▬ HOWARD ZINN, *Declarations of Independence: Cross-Examining American Ideology,* 1990

The function of the historian is to be constantly correcting and completing the image of the past.

▬ DONALD M. DOZER, quoted in *The Vital Past: Writings on the Uses of History* by Stephen Vaughn, 1985

That depends, Henry, on who writes the history.

▬ President RICHARD NIXON, comment to Secretary of State Henry Kissinger after announcing his resignation on August 8, 1974 [According to *RN: The Memoirs of Richard Nixon* (1978), Nixon made this remark after Kissinger tried to console him by saying that history would judge him as one of the greatest presidents. Nixon understood that he could do what Winston Churchill did: influence history by writing it himself.]

History will be kind to me, for I intend to write it.

▬ WINSTON CHURCHILL, British prime minister, quoted by Richard Nixon to Barbara Walters, May 8, 1985

The easiest way to change history is to become a historian.

▬ Unattributed quote, cited in *The Official Explanations* by Paul Dickson, 1980

No one has the right to distort the past; no fact, however disagreeable, may be expunged from the record.

▬ WILLIAM MANCHESTER, journalist and historian, *Look,* April 4, 1967

He who tampers with the memory of mankind is a moral criminal.

▬ JAMES T. FARRELL, *James T. Farrell: Literary Essays, 1954–1977* collected and edited by Jack Alan Robbins, 1976

Someone once said that only by coming to grips with our past can we hope to understand the present. True or not, it's a catchy little phrase.

— Peter Gaffney, humorist, *National Lampoon,* March 1984

(For additional related quotes, see also *Research and Scholarship*)

Hoaxes

These people who are trying to discredit me are ruthless, and they will stop at nothing.

— Clifford Irving, shortly before his purported biography of Howard Hughes was revealed to have been a hoax, quoted in *"No Matter How Thin You Slice It, It's Still Baloney"* edited by Jean Arbeiter, 1984

You're the kind of journalist the *Post* needs . . . because you understand people and get a part of their natures in your story.

— Donald Graham, publisher, *Washington Post,* in a memo to reporter Janet Cooke, just before Cooke's 1981 Pulitzer Prize-winning story about an eight-year-old heroin addict was exposed as a fabrication

There were three immediate offers from publishing houses, and within a month Plimpton signed a six-figure contract calling for a sixty-five-thousand-word manuscript.

— Bruce Weber, *Esquire,* November 1985, describing the industry's reaction to an April Fool's story that appeared in *Sports Illustrated* that year. The author of the article, George Plimpton, wrote about a fictitious New York Mets pitcher, Hayden (Sidd) Finch, who was supposedly a Harvard dropout, and an aspiring monk who spent a year in Tibet, and who possessed an amazing 168-mile-per-hour fastball. Some sportswriters never caught on.

There will be an unremitting emphasis on sex. True excellence in writing will be quickly blue-penciled into oblivion.

— MIKE McGRADY, *Newsday* columnist, instructions to his fellow staffers when they collaborated (in 1970) on a novel, *Naked Came the Stranger* (McGrady set out to prove that a deliberately poorly written sexy novel could sell. He was right, and once the hoax was revealed, the publicity helped rocket the book to the best-seller list.)

We thought the satire obvious, but we have been wrong before, and booksellers across the country have been besieged with orders for Lebouef. Although sorry about that, we are restraining the market urge to talk to a ghostwriter friend about whipping out something to fill the demand.

— Apologia in the February 1967 issue of *Ramparts* for publishing a review of a book that never existed: *Time of Assassins,* supposedly written by one Ulov G. K. Lebouef. The review, by Jacob Brackman and Faye Levine, was intended to spoof the silliness in much of the literature on the Kennedy assassination. Some readers took the review literally; others were offended. According to a book by Brackman, *The Put-on* (1971), one assassination expert, Edward J. Epstein, "said it was one of the funniest things he'd ever read."

I am 100% convinced that Hitler wrote every word in those books . . . [This is] the journalistic scoop of the post–World War II period.

— PETER KOCH, *Stern* editor, on the forged Hitler diaries, April 22, 1983

To be sure, the attention was mixed, and more than a little skepticism accompanied the first news about the diaries' discovery and their immediate publication. Nothing sells like controversy, though, and it quickly became clear that the market could make good use of any early doubts that were to be raised about the authenticity of the new Hitler material.

— ALLAN H. ROSENFELD, *Imagining Hitler*, 1985

How to Get Published (Advice)

Do you realize what would happen if Moses were alive today? He'd go up to Mount Sinai, come back with the Ten Commandments, and spend the next eight years trying to get published.

— ROBERT ORBEN, *The Encyclopedia of One-Liner Comedy,* 1971

The odds against an unknown writer getting a manuscript published by simply sending it directly to a publishing house are astronomical.

— EDWIN MCDOWELL, **publishing correspondent,** *The New York Times,* January 29, 1982

Few of the major trade publishers will take a chance on a manuscript from someone whose name is not known.

— WALTER W. POWELL, *Getting into Print: The Decision-Making Process in Scholarly Publishing,* 1985

Formal channels of manuscript submission are the very last resort of would-be authors . . . To get a book published, recommendation through an informal circle or network is close to being an absolute necessity.

— LEWIS COSER, CHARLES KADUSHIN, and WALTER W. POWELL, *Books: The Culture and Commerce of Publishing,* 1982 (**What these sociologists are trying to say is that an author has to find an agent or another author willing to recommend the manuscript. The authors suggest this will improve the chances of getting published from over one in a thousand to approximately one in ten.**)

If you can get the right idea in front of the right person at the right publishing house . . . you will find that most publishers, far from being unresponsive, will be pursuing you rather than the other way around.

— JOHN BOSWELL, *The Awful Truth About Publishing,* 1986

The young novelist [should try] to obtain the enthusiastic backing of a recognized third party—perhaps a book reviewer or a teacher or another author who might be sufficiently interested to write a publisher, expressing his high opinion of a particular manuscript. Strategically, that puts the young author in the happy position—if the plan works—of being courted by the publisher.

— NORMAN COUSINS, "In Defense of a Writing Career," *The Writer's Craft* edited by John Hersey, 1974

An author should try to get an agent to represent him. Selling a manuscript cold is the toughest way I know to get published. It can be done, but the odds are against the writer.

— WILLIAM TARG, *Indecent Pleasures,* 1975

For better or for worse, agents have increasingly become the keepers of the gates to book-publishing heaven.

— NANCY LOVE, "Everything You Need to Know About Literary Agents," *1995 Writer's Handbook*

It's harder for a new writer to get an agent than a publisher.

— ROGER STRAUS, former president, Farrar, Straus & Giroux, acknowledging the Catch-22 situation that many new writers face, quoted in the *Chicago Sun-Times,* March 30, 1980

In business, contacts are the name of the game. Why, in the art world, are they considered dirty? Getting published is business, too.

— Attributed to BRETT SINGER, author, *The Petting Zoo,* 1979

Something of real quality will be recognized somewhere, sooner or later.

— MIMI JONES, editor, quoted in the *Chicago Sun-Times,* March 30, 1980

It stuns me that people send off their queries and manuscripts blind or to a job title. [A little research on the writer's part would make] a world of difference.

— DAN FRANK, senior editor, Pantheon Books, *1992 Writer's Market*

If I were writing a book, I think I would go down to the local library and read *Publishers Weekly* for a few weeks or months, because I would expect to find an article about an editor which would tell me that my book is for him or that it might not be for him.

—MICHAEL KORDA, editor in chief, Simon & Schuster, quoted in *Writer's Digest*, July 1978

Publishers are always on the lookout for a good book. This is something to keep in mind no matter how discouraging the prospect of finding a publisher is, no matter how many rejection slips you get, and no matter how overwhelming the odds seem.

—RICHARD BALKIN, *A Writer's Guide to Book Publishing*, 1977

It is largely within your power to determine whether a publisher will buy your work and whether the public will buy it once it's released . . . Failures abound because hardly anybody treats getting published as if it were a rational, manageable activity—like practicing law or laying bricks—in which knowledge coupled with skill and application would suffice to ensure success.

—JUDITH APPELBAUM and NANCY EVANS, *How to Get Happily Published*, 1978

Authors do detailed research on their subject matter but seldom do any at all on which publishing house is appropriate for their work.

—WALTER W. POWELL, *Getting Into Print: The Decision-Making Process in Scholarly Publishing*, 1985

Outlets for writing are multiplying rapidly nowadays, as new technology makes small presses and self-publishing ventures economically feasible. And at large houses, as well as small, editorial tastes are always so varied there should be an editor somewhere who's looking for what you have to offer.

—JUDITH APPELBAUM and NANCY EVANS, *How to Get Happily Published*, 1976

Until you have canvassed at least 25–30 publishers you haven't given your book the chance it has to get published.

—RICHARD BALKIN, agent, *Writer's Yearbook 86*

When novice writers ask my advice about getting published, one point I can't emphasize too strongly is the importance of being absolutely relentless about submissions. Once you've got a story to the point where you think it's worth submitting, you must submit it and submit it and submit it until someone somewhere breaks down and buys it.

    — LAWRENCE BLOCK, *Telling Lies for Fun and Profit,* 1981

After twenty commercial publishing houses have turned down a book, I try a small press. When you love a book, you can't give up.

    — ELLEN LEVINE, agent, quoted in *The Writing Business: A Poets & Writers Handbook,* 1985

Literature is like any other trade; you will never sell anything unless you go to the right shop.

    — GEORGE BERNARD SHAW, British playwright, quoted in *Peter's Quotations* by Dr. Laurence J. Peter, 1977

You have to keep writing, keep submitting, and keep praying to the god of whimsy that some editor will respond favorably.

    — Attributed to PETER BENCHLEY, novelist

In the end it's up to you. I'd say that in today's tough publishing climate, you have to want to be a writer very, very much in order to succeed.

    — Attributed to JOSEPH HANSEN, mystery writer

It is not unusual for one editor at a publishing firm to reject a book only to have the same book accepted by another editor . . . Even if the firm turns you down once, you can go back to the other people at the house—assuming, of course, that management has changed or that the book was never presented to the top decision makers in the first place.

    — BILL ADLER, *Inside Publishing,* 1982

The best place to discuss terms with an editor is in bed after a couple of double martinis.

➤ Unidentified female writer, quoted by agent Donald MacCampbell in his book *The Writing Business,* 1978

(See also *Perseverance, Success and Failure, Rejection,* and *Humor*—a large sense of which you will need if you ever deal with publishers. As Michelle Slung noted in her book column in the November 25, 1984 *Washington Post:* "There are hundreds of stories about caterpillarish rejection-slip collectors who turn into best-selling butterflies. In the meantime, a sense of humor and, above all else, patience are qualities it doesn't hurt any aspiring writer to have, while the ability to maintain a certain fatalistic calm is useful, too.")

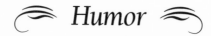 *Humor*

If it's sanity you're after
There's no recipe like
Laughter
Laugh it off.

➤ HENRY RUTHERFORD ELLIOT, quoted in *Barnes & Noble Book of Quotations* edited by Robert I. Fitzhenry, 1983

Now I know laughter is the only correct response. Laughter is self-healing. Laughter is the way I have always borne things . . . Long ago, I discovered laughter is a way of healing your own pain.

➤ NORA EPHRON, director, screenwriter, journalist, and novelist, referring to her painful divorce from Carl Bernstein, which she turned into the novel and screenplay *Heartburn,* 1983

Humor is just another defense against the universe.

➤ MEL BROOKS, filmmaker, quoted in *Barnes & Noble Book of Quotations* edited by Robert I. Fitzhenry, 1983

Laughter is part of the human survival kit.

— DAVID NATHAN, *The Laughtermakers*, 1971

I keep telling young writers I meet that if they want the sure road to success, for heaven's sake, write something that will make people laugh.

— BENNETT CERF, publisher, quoted in *Counterpoint* compiled and edited by Roy Newquist, 1964

Any pundit of even moderate paunch can instruct the Israelites and the Arabs on achieving peace in the Middle East. But to write funny—to write pieces that consistently produce the chuckle or the haw-haw—requires genius of a high order.

— JAMES J. KILPATRICK, *The Writer's Art*, 1984

We respect a person with a sense of humor because a sense of humor means you are in control of a situation. If something can be going terribly wrong and you can find humor in it, it means you are not intimidated by it, and the inference is you can handle it.

— ROBERT ORBEN, gag writer, interview with William A. Gordon, Akron *Beacon Journal*, April 17, 1983

Humor is the secret weapon of the nonfiction writer. It is secret because so few writers realize that it is often their best tool—and sometimes their only tool—for making an important point.

— WILLIAM ZINSSER, *On Writing Well*, 1976

(Humorists) are as serious in purpose as Hemingway or Faulkner— in fact, a national asset in forcing the country to see itself clearly. To them humor is urgent work. It's an attempt to say important things in a special way that regular writers aren't getting said in a regular way—or if they are, it's so regular that nobody is reading it.

— WILLIAM ZINSSER, *On Writing Well*, 1976

The secret source of humor itself is not joy but sorrow.

— MARK TWAIN, *The Mysterious Stranger*, 1922

Humor is one of the ways I cope with the problem of writing novels that generally deal with extremely serious, morbid situations.

➤ JOSEPH HELLER, novelist, quoted in *U.S. News & World Report,* November 12, 1984

In Jewish humor comedy and tragedy are joined together like Siamese twins. "Laughter through tears" is what the Jewish philosopher chooses to call it. You laugh in order to give yourself courage not to grieve; and you shed a tear or two because the human comedy is often no mere laughing matter.

➤ NATHAN AUSUBEL, Introduction to *A Treasury of Jewish Humor,* 1951

Comedy is tragedy plus time.

➤ Attributed to both STEVE ALLEN and LENNY BRUCE

All that means is that something devastating can happen to you today or to your family and all you can do is cry about it or panic or just be grief-stricken about it; but a year or two from now, or maybe ten years from now, or maybe two months or two days, you might be able to see the humor in that problem.

➤ ROBERT ORBEN, gag writer, interview with William A. Gordon, Akron *Beacon Journal,* April 17, 1983

The raw material [of humor] is tragedy . . . It is therefore absurd to assume that there can be such a thing as subject matter totally off-limits to the humorist or comedian.

➤ STEVE ALLEN, *Funny People,* 1981

Against the assault of laughter nothing can stand.

➤ MARK TWAIN, *The Mysterious Stranger,* 1922

I think most of the people you talk to in the humor business had a very unhappy childhood. I once asked George Abbot what he thought made for a creative person and he said, "An unhappy childhood." It makes you go into fantasy very early in life.

➤ ART BUCHWALD, humorist, quoted in *How the Great Comedy Writers Create Laughter* by Larry Wilde, 1976

Truly good humor . . . is bound to offend, for in the nature of things, it ridicules our prejudices and popular institutions.

━ MORDECAI RICHLER, Introduction to *The Best of Modern Humor,* 1984

Good taste and humor are a contradiction in terms . . . like a chaste whore.

━ MALCOLM MUGGERIDGE, *Time,* September 14, 1953

There must be courage; there must be no awe . . . There must be a disciplined eye and a wild mind.

━ DOROTHY PARKER, definition of humor, quoted in her obituary, *The New York Times,* June 8, 1967

Generally speaking, I don't believe in kindly humor—I don't think it exists. One of the most shameful utterances to stem from the human mouth is Will Rogers's "I never met a man I didn't like."

━ S. J. PERELMAN, humorist, quoted in *The New York Times Book Review,* August 9, 1987

[*Definition*] Humor is emotional chaos remembered in tranquility.

━ JAMES THURBER, humorist, quoted in the *New York Post,* February 29, 1960

Humor is an affirmation of dignity, a declaration of man's superiority to all that befalls him.

━ ROMAIN GARY, *Promise at Dawn,* 1961

Humor, in its simplest form, is the unexpected . . . The conjoining of unlikely elements.

━ S. J. PERELMAN, humorist, quoted in *Conversations* by Roy Newquist, 1967

If I think it's funny, it's funny. I don't ever try to think, does anyone think it's funny?

━ FRAN LEBOWITZ, humorist, 1983 interview with William A. Gordon

You have a mongrel perception of humor, nothing more; a multitude of you possess that. This multitude sees the comic side of a thousand low-grade and trivial things—broad incongruities, mainly; grotes-queries, absurdities, evokers of the horselaugh. The ten thousand high-grade comicalities which exist in the world are sealed from their dull vision.

➤ MARK TWAIN, *The Mysterious Stranger*, 1922

There are some great, great humorists sniveling in the bulrushes of America, hiding from their natural enemy, all those unappreciative clods who never get the point of either wild or sophisticated humor. More Americans go to college than ever before, and yet fewer Americans than ever before have the necessary modicum of education and refinement of taste and wit to appreciate satire. In blunt terms, it means they don't get the joke so they don't buy the book so that not-so-dumb publisher stops publishing them and the geniuses either never get into print or they don't stay there long.

➤ WILLIAM PETER BLATTY, novelist, quoted in *Counterpoint* compiled and edited by Roy Newquist, 1964

Contemporary humorists, away from their publishing work, tend to be a most melancholy, even morose lot.

➤ MORDECAI RICHLER, Introduction to *The Best of Modern Humor*, 1984

They did not beat me as a child or as an adult.

➤ FRAN LEBOWITZ in response to William A. Gordon's interview question: "Did your parents ever beat you when you were a child?" (After Lebowitz said she did not understand the question, Gordon commented, "I was really asking why you are funny . . . See, I thought you were going to answer, 'What's a childhood?' or something like that.")

The difference between humor and satire is largely in their purpose. The purpose of humor is to provide the reader with pleasure and relaxation. The purpose of satire is to point out something that is wrong, perhaps even endangering the human race.

➤ Attributed to RICHARD ARMOUR, humorist

Not only have I always been in a state of rage, but I genuinely don't understand why everyone isn't . . . It's the only logical response to life . . . There is a very thin line that divides the comic writer from the mass murderer, and you know, I really have that impulse all the time. So I guess writing or making wisecracks and jokes is a way of not ending up in prison.

— FRAN LEBOWITZ, humorist, interview, *Contemporary Authors,* New Revision series, volume 14, edited by Linda Metzger, 1985

It's a very difficult, competitive job, and I'd say don't do it. Don't ever do it.

— MEL BROOKS, advice to aspiring comedy writers, quoted in *How the Great Comedy Writers Create Laughter* by Larry Wilde, 1976

A humorist entertains his readers. A satirist makes them think.

— RICHARD ARMOUR, humorist, quoted in *Literary Voices* by Jeffrey M. Elliot, 1980

(For additional related quotes, see also *Satire; Wit*)

Ideas

The telephone book is full of facts, but it doesn't contain a single idea.

— MORTIMER J. ADLER, author, quoted in *Barnes & Noble Book of Quotations* edited by Robert I. Fitzhenry, 1983

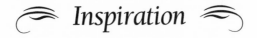

Inspiration

If one waits for the right time to come before writing, the right time never comes.

— JAMES RUSSELL LOWELL, poet and critic, letter to Charles Eliot Norton, April 22, 1883

Writing a novel is like building a wall brick by brick; only amateurs believe in inspiration.

— Attributed to FRANK YERBY, novelist

Writing is a craft with learned skills. There is nothing very mysterious about a lot of it. You must, to be professional, respect craftsmanship and give up mystical baloney about "inspiration" and other stuff that doesn't exist except in the fevered imagination of a few deluded English teachers.

— JACK M. BICKHAM, *Writing and Selling Your Novel,* 1996

I write when I'm inspired, and I see to it that I'm inspired at nine o'clock every morning.

— PETER DE VRIES, novelist, quoted in *The Writer,* June 1994

 *Insults, Memorable*

From the moment I picked up your book until I laid it down I was convulsed with laughter. Someday I intend to read it.

— GROUCHO MARX, comedian, referring to *Dawn Ginsbergh's Revenge* by S. J. Perelman, 1929, quoted in *Life,* February 9, 1962

Some laughter was heard in the back rows [of the theater]. Someone must have been telling jokes back there.

— Attributed to ROBERT BENCHLEY, humorist, reviewing an unfunny play

This is not a novel to be tossed aside lightly. It should be thrown with great force.

— DOROTHY PARKER, critic, quoted in *Wit's End* edited by Robert E. Dremman, 1973

Take an idiot man from a lunatic asylum and marry him to an idiot woman, and the fourth generation of this connection should be a good publisher from an American point of view.

— MARK TWAIN, novelist, quoted in *Memoirs of a Publisher* by F. N. Doubleday, 1972 (Of course, as Robert Hendrickson pointed out in his delightful book, *The Literary Life and Other Curiosities*, Twain later became a publisher himself.)

That's not writing, that's typing.

— TRUMAN CAPOTE, novelist, appraising Jack Kerouac's work, TV interview with David Susskind, *Open End*, 1959

I have nothing to say.

— REED SMOOT, senator from Utah

I know. Now, let's get down to the interview.

— HEYWOOD BROUN, journalist

 *Investigative Reporting*

[*Definition*] An investigative reporter is one who doesn't know when to quit.

— Attributed to DOUGLAS KENNEDY, editor, *True* magazine

An ordinary reporter is persistent. An investigative reporter never gives up, no matter how insurmountable the obstacles, or how hopeless the prospects.

— JAMES DYGERT, *The Investigative Journalist: Folk Heroes of a New Era*, 1976

The new American folk hero . . . The glamour boy of journalism.

— *New York* magazine, referring to the investigative reporter in its November 12, 1973 issue

In a sense, all reporting is investigative, but the phrase "investigative reporting" usually describes sustained attempts to uncover illegal activities or conflicts of interest.

— TOM GOLDSMITH, *The News at Any Cost,* 1985

An investigative reporter has to be a detective, a lawyer, and a social reformer all wrapped up in one, and that's rare.

— A. M. ROSENTHAL, managing editor, *The New York Times,* quoted in *New York* magazine, November 12, 1973

We are pretty good at investigating and nailing someone who is guilty. When we set our minds to it, we can do that, but we never find anyone innocent. If we can't verify an accusation, we just go on to the next one. I'm not sure that is the way it should be.

— BOB WOODWARD, reporter, *Washington Post,* quoted in *The Other Side of the Story* by Jody Powell, 1984

It's almost a perverse pleasure. I like going out and finding something that is going wrong or something that isn't the way people are saying it is, and then putting it in the newspaper.

— BOB WOODWARD, reporter, *Washington Post,* quoted in *The New Muckrakers* by Leonard Downie, Jr., 1976

The investigative reporter serves as a kind of moral custodian of the Republic, trying to close the gap—always there and often wide—between what men say and what men do. Wrongdoing is his target.

— THOMAS POWERS, author and journalist, quoted in *The Nation,* November 6, 1981

We don't have enough of those. It's a shame we have to be nostalgic about them.

— VICTOR NAVASKY, editor, *The Nation,* quoted just 12 years later, *Vanity Fair,* March 1985

Despite the more heroic claims of the news media, daily journalism is largely concerned with finding and retaining profitable sources of packaged stories.

— EDWARD J. EPSTEIN, *Between Fact and Fiction,* 1975

America seems to have entered a phase of counterjournalism led by newspapers themselves. The anger and indignation that once moved reporters to uncover the crimes of the powerful have turned on those who challenge power's prerogatives.

— ALAN WOLFE, *The Nation,* March 24, 1984

We live in this bland yuppified era when people just care about fresh-squeezed orange juice and watching the stock numbers in the paper.

— CHARLES LEWIS, head of the Center for Public Integrity, explaining why investigative journalism is not as valued as it was a generation ago, quoted in *The New York Times,* June 7, 1998

A sustaining myth of journalism holds that every great government scandal is revealed through the work of enterprising reporters who by one means or another pierce the official veil of secrecy. The role that government institutions play in exposing official misconduct and corruption therefore tends to be seriously neglected, if not wholly ignored.

— EDWARD J. EPSTEIN, *Between Fact and Fiction,* 1975

Fewer than fifteen [of the 133 Washington newspaper correspondents] were assigned fulltime to Watergate—some for only two weeks.

— BEN BAGDIKIAN, media critic, arguing that the press as an institution, while taking credit for helping crack the Watergate cover-up, did not perform as admirably as it claimed, *Columbia Journalism Review,* January/February 1973

The most essential gift for a good writer is a built-in, shockproof shit detector. This is the writer's radar and all great writers have had it.

— ERNEST HEMINGWAY, novelist, quoted in *The Paris Review,* Spring 1958

(For additional related quotes, see also *Newswriting and Journalism*)

Irony

There will be no proof that I was ever a writer.

—FRANZ KAFKA, novelist, just before he died in 1924, quoted in *Uncommon Sense: The World's Fullest Compendium of Wisdom* by Joseph Teluskhim, 1987

It isn't a book that I would gamble on for a big sale.

—GEORGE ORWELL, writing to his publisher about his novel *1984*, quoted in *George Orwell: The Road to 1984* by Peter Lewis, 1981 (Orwell certainly was not prescient in this respect. The novel sold over 10 million copies and became a bestseller again in 1984.)

She is a painfully dull, inept, clumsy, undisciplined, rambling and thoroughly amateurish writer whose every sentence, paragraph and scene cries for the hand of a pro.

—DON PRESTON, editor, reaction to the first draft of Jacqueline Susann's *Valley of the Dolls*, 1966, the most popular novel of modern times

Telling Right From Wrong

—Title of a 1985 book on moral philosophy that Random House intended to publish until it was discovered that its author, Timothy J. Cooney, forged a letter of recommendation. The book was subsequently published by Prometheus Books.

Deficient in irony.

—Humorist FRAN LEBOWITZ's opinion of scientists, *Metropolitan Life*, 1978

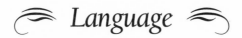

Language

All the fun's in how you say a thing.

— Attributed to ROBERT FROST, poet

One sign of the born writer is his gift for finding or (sometimes) inventing authentically interesting language.

— JOHN GARDNER, *On Becoming a Novelist,* 1983

A huge vocabulary is not always an advantage. Simple language . . . can be more effective than complex language, which can lead to stiltedness or suggest dishonesty or faulty education.

— JOHN GARDNER, *The Art of Fiction,* 1983

One of the most common and erroneous ideas is that the clever writer hides his meaning. In fact, the good writer makes his meaning as clear as possible. He leaves no doubt about what is being read and he is not vague except when he has good reason.

— GARY PROVOST, *Writer's Digest,* March 1984

Edward M. Yoder, former editor of the editorial page of the *Washington Star,* once said that among writers, an addiction to big words is worse than addiction to alcohol. No cure is known to exist. Once the young writer succumbs to arcane polysyallables, he remains syntactically stewed. His rhetorical bibulousness can no longer be restrained. He cannot get enough. He begins to invent words.

— JAMES KILPATRICK, *The Writer's Art,* 1984

The best writing is that which doesn't call attention to itself.

— WILLIAM APPEL and DENISE STERRS, *The Truth About Fiction Writing,* 1997

If it can't be read aloud, it's no good.

— JOHN BRAINE, *Writing a Novel,* 1974

No one can write decently who is distrustful of the reader's intelligence, or whose attitude is patronizing.

— E. B. WHITE, essayist and novelist, quoted in *How to Enjoy Writing* by Janet Asimov and Isaac Asimov, 1987

Never use a metaphor, simile or other figure of speech which you are used to seeing in print; never use a long word where a short one will do; if it is possible to cut a word out always cut it out; never use the passive where you can use the active; never use a foreign phrase, scientific word or jargon word if you can think of an everyday English equivalent.

— Novelist GEORGE ORWELL's rules for writing, quoted in *George Orwell: The Road to 1984* by Peter Lewis, 1981

The purpose of language is to express, not to impress.

— PATRICIA WESTHEIMER, business writing instructor, quoted in *Home Office Computing*, January 1990

A work of art that one has to explain fails . . . its mission.

— HENRY JAMES, *The Art of Fiction and Other Essays*, 1948

The purpose of a story . . . is not to fulfill some crazy formalistic Aristotelian rule, but to get the fucking reader to read the fucking book.

— ERICA JONG, quoted in *Interviews With Contemporary Novelists* by Diana Cooper-Clark, 1986

I've put in so many enigmas and puzzles that it will keep the professors busy for centuries arguing over what I meant.

— Attributed to JAMES JOYCE, novelist, who claimed "that's the only way of insuring one's immortality"

A first-rate writer . . . respects writing too much to be tricky.

— VIRGINIA WOOLF, English novelist, criticizing Joyce's *Ulysses*, in *A Writer's Diary* edited by Leonard Woolf, 1922

It is impossible for a muddy thinker to write good English.

— WILLIAM ZINSSER, *On Writing Well*, 1976

The difference between the right word and the almost right word . . . is the difference between lightning and the lightning bug.

── MARK TWAIN, novelist, quoted in *The Art of Authorship* by
George Bainton, 1890

(For additional related quotes, see also *Word Economy*)

 *Literature*

Literary success of any enduring kind is made by refusing to do what publishers want, by refusing to write what the public wants, by refusing to accept any popular standards, by refusing to write anything to order.

── LAFCADIO HEARN, (who's he?), quoted in *The Life and Letters of*
Lafcadio Hearn edited by Elizabeth Bisland, 1906

Painstaking research proves that one of America's greatest authors may in fact have been readable.

── *National Lampoon,* article headline, January 1984

[*Definition*] "Literature" is written material that, 100 years after the death of the author, is forced upon high school students.

── TOM CLANCY, "How to Write a Bestselling Novel," *Writer's*
Digest, October 1987

Literature is the art of writing something that will be read twice.

── CYRIL CONNOLLY, *Enemies of Promise,* 1938

The business of literature is to reveal life.

── MAXWELL E. PERKINS, letter to Nancy Hale, October 21, 1942,
quoted in *Editor to Author: The Letters of Maxwell E. Perkins*
selected and edited by John Hall Wheelock, 1950

Basically, it is a means of transmitting experience, feeling, and emotion so that one man can tell others, either in the present or in the future, something of the story of how men and women have lived and felt and thought.

— JAMES T. FARRELL, *James T. Farrell: Literary Essays, 1954–1977* collected and edited by Jack Alan Robins, 1976

Literature is, perhaps, the most powerful of the arts.

— JAMES T. FARRELL, *James T. Farrell: Literary Essays, 1954–1977* collected and edited by Jack Alan Robins, 1976

Literature transmits incontrovertible condensed experience from generation to generation.

— ALEXANDER SOLZHENITSYN, Russian writer, Nobel Prize acceptance speech, 1972

The only test of a work of literature is that it shall please other ages than its own.

— GERALD BRENAN, *Thoughts in a Dry Season,* 1978

Maybe the whole idea of the "classic," the book that survives over time, is obsolete; in a society where so much is disposable, why should literature be made to last?

— JAMES ATLAS, *Vanity Fair,* October 1985

One has to face the fact that literature isn't, of necessity, permanent.

— Attributed to CYRIL CONNOLLY, British critic

Literature bores me. I have the impression that it leads nowhere, that literature isn't important.

— EUGENE IONESCO, French playwright, quoted in *Words and Their Masters* by Israel Shenker, 1974

Literature is the orchestration of platitudes.

— THORNTON WILDER, playwright/novelist, quoted in *Time,* January 12, 1953

Literature stirs the mind. It makes you think about a million things, but it does not lead you. So the basic function of literature, as far as I can see, is to entertain the spirit . . . It's basically an entertainment and it has only qualities of entertainment—which means, if you are not entertained while you read a book there is no other reward for you.

> ← ISAAC BASHEVIS SINGER, short-story writer/novelist, quoted in *The Contemporary Writers: Interviews With Sixteen Novelists and Poets* edited by L. S. Dembo and Cyrena Pondrum, 1972

Fiction, even at its best, is remarkably useless in the world of events . . . The men who tinker with rubber, metal, neutrons and drugs—not those who tinker with fiction—hold the key to events.

> ← WRIGHT MORRIS, *About Fiction*, 1975

Writers were not born to change the world. We cannot [even] make it worse.

> ← ISAAC BASHEVIS SINGER, short story writer/novelist, quoted in *Interviews With Contemporary Novelists* by Diana Cooper-Clark, 1986

We have the power to bore people long after we are dead.

> ← SINCLAIR LEWIS, novelist, quoted in *The Complete Guide to Writing Fiction* by Barnaby Conrad, 1980

It seems that the postwar crop of writers has been preoccupied with personal problems. A contemplation of the navel, as it were.

> ← VAN ALLEN BRADLEY, literary critic, quoted in *Conversations* by Roy Newquist, 1967

There are a lot of good writers, but they're not changing anything in American life. They are writing for each other.

> ← NORMAN MAILER, novelist, quoted in the *Los Angeles Times*, May 27, 1998

He knew everything about literature except how to enjoy it.

> ← JOSEPH HELLER, *Catch-22*, 1961

There has been a swing away from the great literature of the twenties and thirties where writers were driven by social injustices of their times.

➤ LEON URIS, novelist, essay "About Exodus," in *The Quest for Truth* edited by Martha Boaz, 1961–1967

If this thirty-year period (1945–1975) has in fact produced its identifying masterpieces, we do not appear to know what they are or where exactly to find them.

➤ WARNER BERTHOFF, *A Literature Without Qualities: American Writing Since 1945*, 1979

Perhaps the times are no longer propitious to the production of masterpieces which both embrace and enhance life.

➤ ANTHONY BURGESS, *The Novel Now*, 1967

This country is crawling with young angry men—in sociology, in politics, in biology. But I am looking for the angry men in literature. I am waiting for a strong spiritual man who would bang his fist on the table and say, "Enough of this nonsense!"

➤ ISAAC BASHEVIS SINGER, short-story writer/novelist, quoted in *The Atlantic Monthly*, July 1970

Let us reflect whether there be any living writer whose silence we would consider a literary disaster.

➤ CYRIL CONNOLLY, British critic, quoted in *Time*, July 26, 1982

Very few disastrous silences loom.

➤ LANCE MORROW, essay "We Need More Writers We'd Miss," *Time*, July 26, 1982 (Morrow named some of the most prominent American writers: John Updike, Joyce Carol Oates, Donald Barthelme, Philip Roth, Joseph Heller, William Styron, John Irving, Norman Mailer, Gore Vidal, and the since deceased John Gardner, Truman Capote, and Walker Percy, and suggested it would not be a cultural disaster if any of them stopped writing.)

Escapist literature at least does much to keep us out of mischief.

➤ MARJORIE BOULTON, *The Anatomy of the Novel*, 1975

Perhaps great writers arrive only at certain stages of a civilization. Great writing may be conjured by great injustice.

— LANCE MORROW, essay "We Need More Writers We'd Miss," *Time,* July 26, 1982

To produce a mighty book, you must choose a mighty theme.

— HERMAN MELVILLE, *Moby Dick,* 1851

No great work has ever been produced except after a long interval of still and musing meditation.

— Attributed to WALTER BAGEHOT, English economist and journalist

The whole game has become one of covering pages with ink, and if literature has become an industry we're lost . . . We have to create literary birth control.

— ISAAC BASHEVIS SINGER, short-story writer/novelist, quoted in *The Atlantic Monthly,* July 1970

One cannot help feeling that its guardians sometimes miss the point of literature, which is not to cut gems of flashing and exquisite rarity but to communicate, to convey a meaning, an art, a story, a fantasy, even a mystery, to someone.

— BARBARA TUCHMAN, historian, lecture, "The Book," at the Library of Congress, October 17, 1979

Who are we in the publishing business, or in the library or bookselling or review business, to judge what is substantial and acceptable for others to read? Can't we be tolerant of the apparent insatiable desire of our society for information and diversion and entertainment? Yes, it's our business to recommend and make business decisions about what we will or won't publish and to do our best to give the book-reading and book-buying public what it wants. But judge, jury and executioner or God we're not.

— PEGGY GLENN, author/publisher, *Publishers Weekly,* January 6, 1984

I am on the verge of rage when I listen to certain kinds of academics who believe that literature is really the province of a select few. It's not. Storytelling is as innate to human experience as music, and some of us may feel a fundamental responsibility to recognize that and to seek as wide an audience as is possible.

> ⎯ SCOTT TUROW, novelist, quoted in *Conversations With American Novelists* edited by Kay Bonetti, Greg Michalson, Speer Morgan, Jo Sapp, and Sam Stowers, 1997

Need we totally scorn mere escapism? . . . The trivial novel may be taking someone's mind off illness, injury, the loneliness of old age or the turmoil of adolescence. There are times when human beings need to put their feet up and relax.

> ⎯ MARJORIE BOULTON, *The Anatomy of the Novel*, 1975

The only end of writing is to enable readers to better enjoy life or better . . . endure it.

> ⎯ MARK JACOBSON, novelist and journalist, "For the Money," essay in *Why I Write: Thoughts on the Craft of Fiction* edited by Will Blythe, 1998

Whoever said that books should have redeeming social value? . . . The first amendment says nothing of the kind.

> ⎯ MICHAEL KORDA, editor, *Inside Books*, February 1989

May Western literature grow and prosper in spite of us all.

> ⎯ MARTIN ASHER, former publisher of Long Shadow Books, which brought us such titles as *Who Farted?* (1983) and *Roseanne Roseannadanna's "Hey, Get Back to Work!" Book* (1983), quoted in *Publishers Weekly*, April 20, 1984.

Never pursue literature as a trade.

> ⎯ SAMUEL TAYLOR COLERIDGE, English poet, *Biographia Literaria*, 1817

Newswriting and Journalism

"I don't like newspapers," he said flatly. He detested inexactitude and shallowness.
  ← CARL BERNSTEIN and BOB WOODWARD, referring to "Deep Throat," their infamous anonymous source, *All the President's Men,* 1974

The difference between journalism and literature is that journalism is unreadable and literature is not read.
  ← OSCAR WILDE, *The Critic As Artist,* 1891

Journalism becomes literature when it tells us not just what happened but what it was like.
  ← L. S. KLEPP, *Entertainment Weekly,* August 22/29, 1997

Journalism can only be literature when it's passionate.
  ← MARGUERITE DURAS, *Practicalities,* 1990

Journalism is literature in a hurry.
  ← MATTHEW ARNOLD, English poet/critic, quoted in *Barnes & Noble Book of Quotations* edited by Robert I. Fitzhenry, 1983

[Journalism is] history's sloppy cousin.
  ← CALVIN TRILLIN, *The New Yorker,* January 21, 1980

News is history shot on the wing.
  ← GENE FOWLER, *Skyline,* 1961

Journalism encourages haste . . . and haste is the enemy of art.
  ← JEANNETTE WINTERSON, *Art Objects,* 1995

It's a newspaper's duty to print the news and raise hell.
  ← WILBUR STOREY, editor, *Chicago Times,* 1861

Reporting—which can be admirable in itself—is poles apart from shaping concepts into imagined actions and requires a totally different ordering of mind and language.

> — THORNTON WILDER, playwright and novelist, quoted in *The Paris Review*, Winter 1957

Newspapers have developed what might be called a vested interest in catastrophe. If they can spot a fight, they play up that fight. If they can uncover a tragedy, they will headline that tragedy.

> — HARRY A. OVERSTREET, philosopher, quoted in *Barnes & Noble Book of Quotations* edited by Robert I. Fitzhenry, 1983

Crisis and tragedy are the meat and potatoes of journalism.

> — C. JOHN SOMMERVILLE, *How the News Makes Us Dumb*, 1999

You furnish the pictures and I'll furnish the war.

> — WILLIAM RANDOLPH HEARST, newspaper publisher, ordering artist Frederic Remington to stay in Cuba even though Remington insisted "there is no trouble here," March 1898

Most journalists are relentless voyeurs who see the warts on the world, the imperfections in people and places.

> — GAY TALESE, *The Kingdom and the Power*, 1981

The problem of media in the modern world is not that they don't get their stories right. They too often miss the right stories . . . They cover bad news. They don't cover good news very well or very often.

> — BEN J. WATTENBERG, *The Good News Is the Bad News Is Wrong*, 1984

Bad news is exciting: scandal, war, murder. It is almost always available if you look for it. It sells papers; it increases television ratings.

> — BEN J. WATTENBERG, *The Good News Is the Bad News Is Wrong*, 1984

News is what upsets us or upsets the world.

> — C. JOHN SOMMERVILLE, *How the News Makes Us Dumb*, 1999

The nature of bad news infects the teller.

    ━ WILLIAM SHAKESPEARE, *Antony and Cleopatra,* 1734

All successful newspapers are ceaselessly querulous and bellicose. They never defend anyone or anything if they can help it; if the job is forced upon them, they tackle it by denouncing someone or something else.

    ━ H. L. MENCKEN, *Prejudices,* 1919

The only way to get through the newspaper each day, Russell Baker once wrote, is to ask, "Is this crisis really worth understanding?" Most of the time the answer is no; in the rush of daily journalism, it is difficult to distinguish the important from the merely urgent.

    ━ CHARLES SILBERMAN, *Criminal Violence, Criminal Justice,* 1978

When dealing with a concept such as *important,* one would be well advised to ask: "To whom?"

    ━ FRAN LEBOWITZ, *Metropolitan Life,* 1978

Strictly speaking, the news is informative insofar as it does indeed provide information. Therefore the questions one must ask are:
1. Do I want this information?
2. Do I need this information?
3. What do they expect me to do about it?

    ━ FRAN LEBOWITZ, *Metropolitan Life,* 1978

Of course, it is not the task of the news media to crank out solutions; but with no instructions on how to incorporate what's happening close to home or far away . . . we feel helpless and betrayed.

    ━ RITA DOVE, **former Poet Laureate of the United States, speech at the National Press Club, March 17, 1994**

A newspaper is always a weapon in somebody's hand.

    ━ CLAUD COCKBURN, *In Time of Trouble,* 1956

Journalism consists in saying "Lord Jones Dead" to people who never knew Lord Jones was alive.

— G. K. CHESTERTON, *The Wisdom of Father Brown,* 1941

That is journalism—an ability to meet the challenge of filling the space.

— REBECCA WEST, novelist, *New York Herald Tribune,* April 22, 1956

In our journalism the trivial displaces the momentous because we tend to measure the importance of events by how recently they happened. We have become so obsessed with facts that we have lost all touch with truth.

— TED KOPPEL, ABC-TV newsman, speech to the International Radio and Television Society, October 1985

The business of journalism is to present facts accurately. Those seeking something larger are advised to look elsewhere.

— ROGER ROSENBLATT, *Time,* July 2, 1984

The press is a midden heap, full of bits and pieces of things, some of them true, and maybe valuable, but all of them fragments from which the citizen must construct his own distorted portrait of reality. I object to the idea that somehow the press, the media, are going to provide people with all the necessary answers.

— LEWIS H. LAPHAM, editor, *Harper's* magazine, quoted in "Can the Press Tell the Truth?" *Harper's,* January 1985

The trouble with the news business (OK, one of the troubles) is that reporters have to take seriously the words of famous and/or powerful people, even if said people ought not to be taken seriously.

— JON MARGOLIS, columnist, *Chicago Tribune,* August 1984

It is journalistically "accurate" to report someone else's nonsensical assertions.

— STEPHAN LESHER, *Media Unbound,* 1982

Most press criticism is wondrously off-base . . . The truth is that laziness—the failure to make the extra phone call—accounts for as many media screwups as anything imagined by [its critics].
— DAVID REMNICK, "Scoop," *The New Yorker,* January 29, 1996

Much of our flawed work is never acknowledged or corrected.
— RICHARD HARWOOD, "How Lies See Light of Day," *Washington Post,* July 13, 1998

There is much to be said in favor of modern journalism. By giving us the opinions of the uneducated, it keeps us in touch with the ignorance of the community.
— OSCAR WILDE, *The Complete Works of Oscar Wilde,* 1966

Journalists often act more like stenographers than reporters, richly transcribing lies, half-truths, disinformation, and propaganda without attempting to put remarks in perspective or pointing out when something is amiss.
— MARTIN A. LEE and NORMAN SOLOMON, *Unreliable Sources: A Guide to Detecting Bias in the News Media,* 1990

If truth was a factor, we couldn't publish half the statements public officials make.
— SEYMOUR HERSH, investigative journalist and author, *Rolling Stone,* April 18, 1985

What qualifies journalists to know the truth when they see it? Are they philosophers? Judges? Theologians? Do they have the leisure to reflect upon events and their meaning? Rarely.
— ARTHUR PLOTNIK, *Honk If You're a Writer,* 1992

The highest goal in journalism is to bring someone down . . . It is the way careers and reputations are made.
— JAY ROSEN, associate professor of journalism, New York University, quoted in *U.S. News & World Report,* October 5, 1998

Reporters are like puppets. They simply respond to the pull of the most powerful strings.

— President LYNDON B. JOHNSON, quoted in *Lyndon Johnson & The American Dream* by Doris Kearns, 1976

If the whole truth eludes historians, it certainly is not the domain of the press. Journalists deal with Monday's truth, Tuesday's truth, and if the story holds up, Wednesday's.

— ROGER ROSENBLATT, senior writer, *Time*, commencement address, University of Maryland, Baltimore County, June 3, 1984

When the day dissolves, little, if anything, will be remembered of these things.

— ROGER ROSENBLATT, *Time*, December 12, 1983

The world is full of people who honestly don't know that journalists are not their friends. They honestly have no idea how awful it is to be misquoted or quoted out of context or to have what they said quoted but used to make a point they never intended—all of which, I'm sorry to say, is standard operating procedure among the majority of journalists.

— NORA EPHRON, former journalist and now director, quoted in the *Columbia Journalism Review*, July/August 1989

Let me tell you about our profession. We are the meanest, nastiest bunch of jealous, petty people who ever lived . . . You think I wouldn't sell my mother for My Lai?

— SEYMOUR HERSH, investigative journalist and author, quoted in *Vanity Fair*, November 1997

Every journalist who is not too stupid or too full of himself to notice what is going on knows that what he does is morally indefensible. He is a kind of confidence man, preying on people's vanity, ignorance, or loneliness, gaining their trust and betraying them without remorse.

— JANET MALCOLM, *The Journalist and the Murderer*, 1980

If you do your job right, only two people show up at your funeral.
  — LEWIS LAPHAM, editor, *Harper's,* quoted in the *Los Angeles Times,*
  May 29, 1998

You are going to make enemies all the time if you do your job.
  — GERALD POSNER, quoted in *Raising Hell: Straight Talk With Inves-
  tigative Journalists* edited by Ron Chepesiuk, Haney Howell, and
  Edward Lee, 1997

When I was a young reporter and a young man I wish I would have
been more concerned with the human beings I was writing about
than about getting their stories. I wish my ambition would have
been tempered with more compassion and sensitivity. It's one of
the things that made me want to get out of journalism. As a journalist you mute what you really care about, so that you can cover
those stories. I had a prof in journalism school who said to me,
"You'll know you're really a good reporter when you can go to an
autopsy and eat a cheeseburger while watching it."
  — JOE ESZTERHAS, screenwriter, interview, *Playboy,* April 1998

People who are drawn to journalism are usually people who, because
of their cynicism or emotional detachment or reserve or whatever,
are incapable of becoming anything but witnesses to events.
  — NORA EPHRON, *Wallflower at the Orgy,* 1970

To have integrity in the media business today means only to be "objective," which has become a code word for having no convictions.
  — SUSAN FALUDI, *The Nation,* May 27, 1996

Objectivity is a word that was invented by those who refused to stand
up alone. I do believe that journalism is a fighting profession. You
have to fight. You fight for [a] cause, you fight against corruption,
you fight against misleading information. You fight for a lot of things.
  — DAVID HALEVY, former *Time* magazine correspondent and author
  of *Inside the PLO,* quoted in *Booknotes: America's Finest Authors
  on Reading, Writing and the Power of Ideas,* 1997

Of all the myths of journalism, objectivity is the greatest.

— Attributed to BILL MOYERS, journalist and President Lyndon B. Johnson's press secretary

Reportage, the natural realm of those without creative imagination.

— GORE VIDAL, novelist, interview, *Playboy,* 1969

Working as a journalist is exactly like being a wallflower at the orgy. I always seem to find myself at a perfectly wonderful event where everybody is having a marvelous time, laughing merrily, eating, drinking, having sex in the back room, and I am on the side taking notes on it all.

— NORA EPHRON, *Wallflower at the Orgy,* 1970

Is it too much to ask that the press be on our side?

— LORD CHALFORT, former British foreign secretary, asking why the press covers acts of terrorism objectively

I think all newspaper men are aware of the ephemeral nature of their craft, and want to write something which lasts a little longer.

— Attributed to BOB THOMAS, Hollywood columnist and biographer

For all its faults, journalism is the one institution that preserves free inquiry and therefore freedom itself.

— JAMES DEAKEN, *Straight Stuff,* 1984

 *Novels*

Every journalist has a novel in him, which is an excellent place for it.

— RUSSELL LYNES, former managing editor, *Harper's,* quoted in *Quotations of Wit and Wisdom* by John W. Gardner and Francesca Gardner Reese, 1975

Newspaper work will not harm a young writer and could help him if he gets out of it in time.

━ ERNEST HEMINGWAY, novelist, quoted in *The Paris Review,*
Spring 1958

Journalism allows its readers to witness history; fiction gives its readers the opportunity to live it.

━ JOHN HERSEY, *The Atlantic Monthly,* 1949

In the true novel, as opposed to reportage and chronicle, the main action takes place inside the characters' skull and ribs.

━ ARTHUR KOESTLER, British author, quoted in *The Concise Columbia Dictionary of Quotations* by Robert Andrews, 1989

The historian's view is like that of a jet pilot's who sees the hundreds of cars on a freeway as one great fused mechanical entity. But the novelist, as he writes about our time, will continue to zoom in and focus upon the individual, for he knows—and sometimes the historian doesn't—that in the entire universe there is only one thing that possesses an ultimate importance, and that is the individual.

━ FREDERICK SHROYER, historian, quoted in *The Quest for Truth* by Martha Boaz, 1961–1967

The object of the novel . . . is to enlarge experience, not to convey facts.

━ DAVID GARNETT, British writer, quoted in *Contemporary Novelists* by James Vinson, 1976

A novel is an impression, not an argument.

━ THOMAS HARDY, Preface to *Tess of the D'Urbervilles,* 1891

The purpose of fiction is still, as it was to Joseph Conrad, to make the reader see.

━ PETER DE VRIES, *Without a Stitch in Time,* 1972

In no other vehicle is contemporary life so adequately expressed.

━ FRANK NORRIS, *The Responsibilities of the Novelist,* 1903

I think we should put away the stethoscope and leave the patient alone.

— PETER DE VRIES, novelist, dismissing the debate over whether the novel is dying, quoted in *Conversations* by Roy Newquist, 1967

The fact that Judith Krantz can make three million dollars is proof that the novel is alive and well.

— ERICA JONG, novelist, quoted in *Interviews With Contemporary Novelists* by Diana Cooper-Clark, 1986

Novels seem more expendable these days than ever, but *novelist* is still any writer's notion of original talent.

— ALFRED KAZIN, *Bright Book of Life,* 1973

[*Definition*] The literary form of greatest prestige.

— EDWIN BERRY BURGUM, *The Novel and the World's Dilemma,* 1963

Fiction is nothing less than the subtlest instrument for self-examination and self-display that mankind has invented yet.

— JOHN UPDIKE, *Odd Jobs,* 1991

The idea of a novel should stir your blood.

— PAT CONROY, novelist, "Stories," essay in *Why I Write: Thoughts on the Craft of Fiction* edited by Will Blythe, 1998

Every novel should have a beginning, a muddle and an end.

— Attributed to PETER DE VRIES, novelist

If you would understand your age, read the works of fiction produced by it. People in disguise speak freely.

— ARTHUR HELPS, British author, quoted in *Barnes & Noble Book of Quotations* edited by Robert I. Fitzhenry, 1983

Every novelist has something in common with a spy: he watches, he overhears, he seeks motives and analyzes characters, and in his attempt to serve literature he is unscrupulous.

— GRAHAM GREENE, *Ways of Escape,* 1980

Fiction reveals truths that reality obscures.

➤JESSAMYN WEST, quoted in *Reader's Digest,* April 1973

Reading the *Valley of the Dolls* was like reading a very, very long, absolutely delicious gossip column full of nothing but blind items. The fact that the names were changed and the characters disguised just made it more fun.

➤NORA EPHRON, *Wallflower at the Orgy,* 1970

There is only one trait that marks the writer. He is always watching. It's a kind of trick of the mind and he is born with it.

➤Attributed to MORLEY CALLAGHAN, Canadian writer

For me, the criterion [for a really good novel] is that the author has created a total world in which his people move credibly. The books that do that, I prize very much.

➤JAMES MICHENER, novelist, quoted in *Conversations With Writers II* edited by Matthew J. Bruccoli, 1978

A well-composed book is a magic carpet on which we are wafted to a world that we cannot enter in any other way.

➤CAROLINE GORDON, *How to Read a Novel,* 1964

Good writers are in the business of leaving signposts saying, Tour my world, see and feel it through my eyes; I am your guide.

➤LARRY L. KING, *None but a Blockhead: On Being a Writer,* 1986

As a reader, I want a book to kidnap me into its world. Its world must make my so-called real world seem flimsy. Its world must lure me to return. When I close the book, I should feel bereft.

➤ERICA JONG, "Doing It for Love," *The Writer,* July 1997

The trouble with some contemporary novels is that they are full of people not worth knowing. The characters slide in and out of the mind with hardly a ripple.

➤NORMAN COUSINS, *Human Options,* 1981

For me, a page of good prose is where one hears the rain. A page of good prose is when one hears the noise of battle. A page of good prose has the power to give grief a universality that lends it a youthful beauty. A page of good prose has the power to make us laugh. A page of good prose seems to me the most serious dialogue that well-informed and intelligent men and women carry on today in their endeavor to make sure that the fires of this planet burn peaceably.

—JOHN CHEEVER, novelist, speech accepting the National Medal for Literature, April 27, 1982, quoted in *John Cheever: A Biography* by Scott Donaldson, 1988

A story must be exceptional enough to justify its telling. We story-tellers are all Ancient Mariners, and none of us is justified in stopping Wedding Guests (in other words, the hurrying public), unless he has something more unusual to relate than the ordinary experiences of every average man and woman.

—THOMAS HARDY, *The Early Life of Thomas Hardy*, 1928

A novel needs a single, cohesive theme that operates as the guiding force behind the story. For example, the theme in [my book] *Message in a Bottle* is the question, "Is it possible to fall in love a second time, after losing your one true love?" Everything in the novel—the characters, the plot, the pacing, the style—all revolve around this theme, which helps hold the story together.

—NICHOLAS SPARKS, novelist, quoted in *Writer's Digest*, November 1998

Anyone can think up a story. But trying to breathe life into characters, allow them space, make them people whom I care about is hard.

—PHYLLIS REYNOLDS NAYLOR, *The Craft of Writing the Novel*, 1989

No novel is anything . . . unless the reader can sympathize with the characters whose names he finds upon the pages.

—ANTHONY TROLLOPE, *Autobiography*, 1883

Plot gets readers involved, characterization makes them care.
— PAUL RAYMOND MARTIN, *The Writer's Little Instruction Book,* 1998

When writing a novel a writer should create living people, not characters. A character is a caricature.
— ERNEST HEMINGWAY, *Death in the Afternoon,* 1932

A stick man.
— MALCOLM MCCONNELL, novelist, referring to a fictional character that is not fully flushed, *The Essence of Fiction: A Practical Handbook,* 1986

Character is the "heart of fiction." Before you can become interested in the development and outcome of the conflict in the story, you must care about the main character, the protagonist (who struggles for something).
— DAVID MADDEN, *The Fiction Tutor,* 1996

You must write about people who touch the reader; you must make the reader *care.*
— JOHN IRVING, novelist, quoted in *Conversations on Writing Fiction* by Alexander Neubauer, 1994

Characters that seem to live are the most important single element in the novel. No one remembers novels for their style, or for the skills with which their plots were constructed.
— NANCY HALE, *The Realities of Fiction,* 1962

Live with them [your characters]. Think about them. Visualize them in different environments and in different situations. See how they would react under this stimulus or that and imagine those scenes as if they were scenes in all their details. After you have done this for a few weeks or months, you will have no difficulty in making your characters seem real to your readers, because they will seem real to you.
— MAREN ELWOOD, *Characters Make Your Story,* 1942

Do as the painter or sculptor does; take your models from life.
   — MAREN ELWOOD, *Characters Make Your Story*, 1942

Good characters are not real people; they are better than real people. Good characters are not only exaggerated, but more goal-oriented, more consistent (with tricks used to make them appear more complex than they really are), engaged in more dramatic circumstances than most of us ever encounter in day-to-day living, and more committed to their quest.
   — JACK M. BICKHAM, *Writing and Selling Your Novel*, 1996

From the date of birth until the time the story begins, I know everything about my characters . . . What are their good points and bad points? What are their foibles and eccentricities and how did they get them? . . . Your characters must become as real to you as to your neighbors; if they are not real to you, it's damned sure that they will not be real to your readers.
   — TOM CLANCY, "How to Write a Bestselling Novel," *Writer's Digest*, October 1987

[When I want to] introduce a character—I sort of audition my characters—let's see if they work or not.
   — ELMORE LEONARD, novelist, writing in *The Complete Guide to Writing Fiction* by Barnaby Conrad, 1990

Creating believable backgrounds for characters gave me problems until one day, while filling out a job application form, it hit me. I would make my characters apply to be in my stories. I'd learn about my characters the same way companies learn about new employees: an application form.
   — TOM CLANCY, "How to Write a Bestselling Novel," *Writer's Digest*, October 1987

I'd like to write another book, a novel about the intrigues in the fashion business, and have a dress be the main character.
   — JERRY HALL, model, quoted in *Rolling Stone*, April 25, 1985

I have a 54-point questionnaire I answer about each of the four or five main characters in my books. Physical description, psychological profile, work experience, hobbies, big dreams, and on and on.

— CHET CUNNINGHAM, "How to Write and Sell 200 Novels (by Someone Who Has)," *Writer's Digest,* July 1991

Making the reader like or dislike the character is generally half the battle. Sometimes, as with Raskolnikov in *Crime and Punishment,* we neither like nor dislike the protagonist but we understand him and are interested in his fate.

— BARNABY CONRAD, *The Complete Guide to Writing Fiction,* 1990

I leave out the parts that people skip.

— ELMORE LEONARD, explaining the popularity of his novels, *Publishers Weekly,* March 8, 1985

It is easy enough, once the commercial success of a book is an established fact, to work out a convincing reason for the public's enthusiasm. But, before the fact has happened, the business is mysterious, chancy, [and] unpredictable.

— ELIZABETH HARDWICK, "The Decline of Book Reviewing," in *Writing in America* edited by John Fischer and Robert B. Silvers, 1960

Novels are wild cards. No one knows what makes a novel sell.

—JANE ADAMS, *How to Sell What You Write,* 1984

I find that nonfiction writers are the likeliest to turn out interesting novels.

— Attributed to MICHAEL KORDA, editor in chief, Simon & Schuster

Write a novel if you must, but think of money as an unlikely accident. Get your reward out of writing it, and try to be content with that.

— PEARL BUCK, "Please Tell Me . . . ," essay in *Writer's Roundtable* edited by Helen Hull and Michael Drury, 1959

I'm no Joan Didion. There are no intelligent, unhappy people in my books. I want to be known as a writer of good entertaining narrative. I'm not trying to be taken seriously by the East Coast literary establishment. But I'm taken very seriously by the bankers.

➤ JUDITH KRANTZ, novelist, quoted in *The Blockbuster Complex* by Thomas Whiteside, 1981

 *Originality*

There is nothing new under the Sun.

➤ Ecclesiastes 1:9

The most original authors . . . are not so because they advance what is new, but because they put what they have to say as if it had never been said before.

➤ JOHANN WOLFGANG VON GOETHE, *Spruche in Prosa,* 1819

The original writer is not one who imitates nobody, but one whom nobody can imitate.

➤ FRANÇOIS RENE DE CHATEAUBRIAND, *Le Genie du Christianisme,* 1802

The man is most original who can adapt from the greatest number of sources.

➤ THOMAS CARLYLE, *On Heroes and Hero-Worship and the Heroic in History,* 1840

We are as much informed of a writer's genius by what he selects as by what he originates.

➤ RALPH WALDO EMERSON, essayist, poet, and philosopher, quoted in *Barnes & Noble Book of Quotations* edited by Robert I. Fitzhenry, 1983

A new idea is delicate. It can be killed by a sneer or a yawn; it can be stabbed to death by a quip or worried to death by a frown on the right man's brow.

— CHARLES BROWER, *Advertising Age*, August 10, 1959

Novelty comes chiefly from ingenious genre-crossing or elevation of familiar materials.

— JOHN GARDNER, *The Art of Fiction*, 1983

In publishing, originality can be a drawback, making a novel's artistic merit difficult to judge and its commercial prospects impossible to predict.

— CARYN JAMES, novelist, *The New York Times Book Review*, May 6, 1984

A great book is often ahead of its time, and the trick is how to keep it afloat until the times catch up with it.

— ROBERT GIROUX, chairman, Farrar, Straus & Giroux, quoted in *Wilson Library Bulletin*, March 1982

A good artist predicts as well as reflects, and all I ask is that they say, "We know now what they couldn't see then. He was six months ahead of his time."

— PETER DE VRIES, novelist, quoted in *Conversations* by Roy Newquist, 1967

Every compulsion is put on writers to become safe, polite, obedient and sterile.

— SINCLAIR LEWIS, in a letter declining the Pulitzer Prize for his novel *Arrowsmith*, May 6, 1926

How daring and how dangerous the innovators often seem in their own day! . . . Wait fifty years, and they do not seem so daring or dangerous, so godlike or so devilish.

— ASHLEY THORNDIKE, *The Outlook for Literature*, 1969

The world in general doesn't know what to make of originality; it is startled out of its comfortable habits of thought, and its first reaction is one of anger.

➤ W. SOMERSET MAUGHAM, *Great Novelists and Their Novels*, 1948

All profoundly original work looks ugly at first.

➤ Attributed to CLEMENT GREENBERG, American art critic

One age's oddities and curiosities are often another's masterpieces. It may be that it requires a long absorptive time for a unique style to be understood and then admired, or an original thought to be comprehended and then appreciated. The resistance to such phenomena is great. Most people prefer the easy and familiar . . . Only the future reveres the original and daring style.

➤ DORIS GRUMBACH, Introduction to *Writer's Choice* edited by Linda Sternberg Katz and Bill Katz, 1983

 *Perseverance*

With ordinary talents and extraordinary perseverance all things are attainable.

➤ THOMAS BUXTON, *Memoirs of Sir Thomas Fowell Buxton* edited by Charles Buxton, 1849

Nothing in the world can take the place of perseverance. Talent will not; nothing in this world is more common than men with talent. Genius will not; unrewarded genius is almost a proverb. Education will not; the world is full of educated derelicts. Perseverance and determination alone are omnipotent. The slogan "Press on" has solved and always will solve the problems of the human race.

➤ Attributed to CALVIN COOLIDGE, U.S. president

Our greatest weakness lies in giving up. The most certain way to succeed is always to try just one more time.

— THOMAS EDISON, inventor, quoted in *The World's Best Thoughts on Success & Failure* compiled by Eugene Raudsepp

Everyone thinks they can be a writer. Most people don't understand what's involved. The real writers persevere. The ones that don't, either don't have enough fortitude and they probably wouldn't succeed anyway, or they fall in love with the glamour of writing as opposed to the writing of writing.

— PETER McWILLIAMS, author, quoted in *1984 Writers Market*

The trick is not to give up, ever. Suppose the late Erskine Caldwell had been able to stand only six years of soul-battering rejection. Instead of going on to write some forty books, he would have been a failure, like Victor Borge's uncle who unsuccessfully tried to market a variety of soft drinks called from 1-Up to 6-Up—and then quit.

— BARNABY CONRAD, *The Complete Guide to Writing Fiction,* 1990

With but very few exceptions, every writer whose published work you have read or relished managed to capture your attention only after taking a fearsome beating of the ego.

— GEORGE V. HIGGINS, *On Writing: Advice for Those Who Write to Publish (or Would Like To),* 1990

(For additional related quotes, see also *Success and Failure*)

Plagiarism

Oscar Wilde: Oh, I wish I'd said that.
James Whistler: You will, Oscar, you will.

— Quoted in *Oscar Wilde* by Leonard Cresswell Ingleby, 1907

Your manuscript is both good and original; but the part that is good is not original, and the part that is original is not good.

— SAMUEL JOHNSON, English writer, lexicographer, and critic, quoted in *Rotten Rejections: A Literary Companion* edited by André Bernard, 1990

If you steal from one author it's plagiarism; if you steal from many it's research.

— WILSON MIZNER, entertainer and writer, quoted in *The Legendary Mizners* by Alva Johnston, 1953

If we steal thoughts from the moderns, it will be cried down as plagiarism; if from the ancients, it will be cried up as erudition.

— CHARLES CALEB COLTON, *Lacon,* 1825

Immature artists imitate, mature artists steal.

— LIONEL TRILLING, critic and author, quoted in *Esquire,* September 1962

Immature poets imitate; mature poets steal.

— T. S. ELIOT, *The Sacred Wood: Essays on Poetry and Criticism,* 1920

I think it may be said that the more worthless the manuscript, the greater the fear of plagiarism.

— SIR STANLEY UNWIN, *The Truth About Publishing,* 1926

All writers are thieves; theft is a necessary tool of the trade.

— NINA BAWDEN, *Mothers: Reflections by Daughters,* 1998

It doesn't matter who says it first, it's who gets credit for it last that counts.

— Attributed to OSCAR LEVANT, actor

The only "ism" she believes in is plagiarism.

— DOROTHY PARKER, humorist, speaking of a well-known author, quoted in her obituary, *Publishers Weekly,* June 19, 1967.

Good swiping is an art in itself.
— JULES FEIFFER, *Ackroyd*, 1988

This is something you never, never do. Every line of work needs clear rules. If you're a soldier, you don't desert. If you're a writer, you don't steal anyone's prose. It should be the one [cause for] automatic firing.
— JAMES FALLOWS, Washington editor of *The Atlantic Monthly*, quoted in *Columbia Journalism Review*, July/August 1995

 *Poetry*

There's no money in poetry, but there's no poetry in money either.
— ROBERT GRAVES, poet/novelist, speech, London School of Economics, December 6, 1963

It's a sad fact about our culture that a poet can earn much more money writing or talking about his art than he can by practicing it.
— W. H. AUDEN, *The Dyer's Hand*, 1962

The only serious poet in this century said to have been able to live off his poetry was Robert Frost.
— JOSEPH EPSTEIN, *Plausible Prejudices*, 1985

Among America's 240 million people there aren't 1,000 who want a book of poetry badly enough to pay the price of a small pizza for it.
— BEVERLY JARRETT, associate director, Louisiana State University Press, quoted in the *Chronicle of Higher Education*, June 26, 1985

Poetry is living proof that rhyme doesn't pay.
— Anonymous

Can you imagine thousands of American men and women crowding into Yankee Stadium to hear Robert Lowell or James Dickey read his poems? Yet we are told that such things have actually happened in Soviet Russia.

— JAY B. HUBBELL, *Who Are the Major American Writers?*, 1972

In America . . . the only poets with full-time salaries earn them at greeting-card companies.

— BILL THOMAS, *Los Angeles Times,* January 13, 1991

Publishing a volume of poetry is like dropping a rose petal down the Grand Canyon and waiting for the echo.

— DON MARQUIS, *Sun Dial Time,* 1936

Poet: A person born with the instinct to poverty.

— ELBERT HUBBARD, *The Roycroft Dictionary and Book of Epigrams,* 1923

To be a poet is a condition rather than a profession.

— ROBERT GRAVES, English poet and novelist, in answer to a question, *Horizon* magazine

For a man to become a poet . . . he must be in love or miserable.

— LORD BYRON, *Conversations of Lord Byron* edited by Ernest J. Lovell, Jr., 1969

Almost all good women poets are either divorced or lesbians.

— ROBERT LOWELL, poet, quoted in *San Francisco Chronicle,* May 25, 1977

The purpose of poetry is to contribute to man's happiness.

— WALLACE STEVENS, poet, quoted in *Can Poetry Matter?* by Dana Gioia, 1992

Poetry is the record of the best and happiest moments of the happiest and best minds.

— PERCY BYSSHE SHELLEY, *A Defence of Poetry,* 1821

Poetry is a way of taking life by the throat.

— ROBERT FROST, poet, quoted in *Robert Frost: The Trial by Existence* by Elizabeth Shepley Sergeant, 1960

The mission of the poet is to soothe.

— REBECCA HARDING DAVIS, *Waiting for the Verdict,* 1968

All the good wedding poems in the world could be scribbled on a placard. Poets love grief.

— D. J. BRUCKNER, "Epithalamiums," *The New York Times Book Review,* May 15, 1983

A poet looks at the world as a man looks at a woman.

— WALLACE STEVENS, *Opus Posthumous: Adagia,* 1957

Genuine poetry can communicate before it is understood.

— T. S. ELIOT, *Dante,* 1929

I've written some poetry I don't understand myself.

— Attributed to CARL SANDBURG, poet

Poetry can communicate the actual quality of experience with a subtlety and precision unapproachable by any other means.

— F. R. LEWIS, *New Bearings in English Poetry,* 1932

Unless it enraptures it is not poetry.

— JOSEPH JOUBERT, *Pensees,* 1842

Poetry is the language in which man explores his own amazement.

— CHRISTOPHER FRY, British dramatist, quoted in *Time,* April 3, 1950

A poet is, before anything else, a person who is passionately in love with language.

— W. H. AUDEN, poet and dramatist, quoted in *The New York Times,* October 9, 1960

A poet can survive anything but a misprint.

➤ OSCAR WILDE, *The Complete Works of Oscar Wilde,* 1966

Poetry lifts the veil from behind the hidden beauty of the world.

➤ PERCY BYSSHE SHELLEY, *A Defence of Poetry,* 1821

A poem is no place for an idea.

➤ EDGAR W. HOWE, *Country Town Sayings,* 1911

If Galileo had said in verse that the world moved, the Inquisition would have left him alone.

➤ THOMAS HARDY, English novelist, quoted in *The Later Years of Thomas Hardy* by F. E. Hardy, 1930

A poet who reads his verse in public may have other nasty habits.

➤ ROBERT HEINLEIN, *Time Enough for Love: The Lives of Lazarus Long,* 1978

In no other job have I ever had to deal with such utterly abnormal people. Yes, it is true, poetry does something to them.

➤ MURIEL SPARK, on working for England's Poetry Society, *Curriculum Vitae*

 *Posterity, Writing for*

If you would not be forgotten, as soon as you are dead and rotten, either write things worth reading, or do things worth the writing.

➤ BENJAMIN FRANKLIN, *Poor Richard's Almanac,* 1738

To be remembered after we are dead is but poor recompense for being treated with contempt while we are living.

➤ WILLIAM HAZLITT, *Characteristics,* 1821–1822

Posterity—what you write for after being turned down by publishers.
— GEORGE ADE, *Forty Modern Fables,* 1901

There is something touching in the firm trust every author of a flop puts in posterity.
— KURT TUCHOLSKY, *Gesammelte Werke,* 1975

Posterity—an appellate court which reverses the judgment of a popular author's contemporaries, the appellant being his obscure competitor.
— AMBROSE BIERCE, *The Devil's Dictionary,* 1911

Whenever an artist thinks that the community does not sufficiently appreciate him, he takes an appeal to posterity. I wonder where his notion comes from, that posterity is equipped with superior judgment and wisdom.
— HEYWOOD BROUN, *Sitting on the World,* 1924

What every author hopes to receive from posterity—a hope usually disappointed—is justice.
— W. H. AUDEN, *Selected Poetry and Prose,* 1966

Posterity is as likely to be as wrong as anyone else.
— HEYWOOD BROUN, *Sitting on the World,* 1924

Why should people be less stupid tomorrow than they are today?
— JULES RENARD, *Journal,* 1887

How much of the work of the 1600's is still around except Shakespeare's?
— SAMUEL Z. ARKOFF, producer of *I Was a Teenage Werewolf* and other so-called B movies, quoted in *People,* October 15, 1979

Humans are generally reluctant to paw through last week's garbage on the off chance of finding the lost penny or two.
— BRYAN F. GRIFFIN, *Harper's,* September 1981

Dead manuscripts tell no tales.

➤ AMBROSE BIERCE, 1909 essay, "Some Disadvantages of Genius"

Immortality depends on promotion, not on literary genius.

➤ DEAN POWELL, critic, quoted in *Who Are the Major American Writers?* by Jay B. Hubbell, 1972

Books are a form of immortality. The words of men whose bodies are dust still live in their books . . . All the great lives that have lived have been told about in books.

➤ WILFRED A. PETERSON, *The Art of Living by Day,* 1972

They are not dead, those people. The writers of books do not truly die; their characters, even the ones who throw themselves in front of trains or are killed in battle, come back to life over and over again.

➤ ANNA QUINDLEN, *How Reading Changed My Life,* 1998

He [the writer] knows he has a short span of life, that the day will come when he must pass through the walls of oblivion, and he wants to leave a scratch on the wall—Kilroy was here—that somebody a hundred, or a thousand years later will see.

➤ WILLIAM FAULKNER, quoted in *Writers at Work,* First Series, 1958

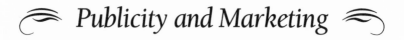 *Publicity and Marketing*

The most difficult of all [tasks] that a mortal man can embark on is to sell a book.

➤ SIR STANLEY UNWIN, *The Truth About Publishing,* 1926

Persuading a customer to part with $7.95, $10.00, or $15.00 for a new book is an act of magic, in my opinion.

➤ WILLIAM TARG, *Indecent Pleasures,* 1975

The main difference between marketing a book and marketing soap is that a book is a one-shot deal . . . and a book usually only has 90 days to make it or it's dead.

— CAROLE DOLPH, former promotional manager, Doubleday & Co., interview with *Publishers Weekly*

Somewhere between milk and yogurt.

— CALVIN TRILLIN, on the average shelf life of a book, *Uncivil Liberties*, 1982

Call it the curse of abundance; with roughly 35,000 new books each year and periodicals standing up all the time, only a small percentage of what's published catches the attention of the public.

— JUDITH APPELBAUM and NANCY EVANS, *How to Get Happily Published*, 1976

The struggle in publishing . . . is to get attention in a crowded marketplace.

— SIMON MICHAEL BESSIE, editor, quoted in *U.S. News & World Report*, December 5, 1983

We are now fighting not for the book, but for attention. You are asking people to go into a bookstore because they've heard something about your book and then give 5 to 10 hours of their time reading it. It's a struggle to attract readers because of all the other distractions in the country. You're like a little child saying, "Listen to me, Mommy."

In a way it makes you feel slimy. You want your book to be discovered for itself, and instead you find yourself pleading for it.

— THEODORE WHITE, historian, quoted in *The New York Times*, July 24, 1982

Everything in this world has turned into show business. Politics is show business. Running Chrysler is show business . . . Sports is show business, and Henry Kissinger is show business . . . And if you're not in show business, you're really off Broadway.

— FELIX ROHAYTN, investment banker, quoted in *The Blockbuster Complex* by Thomas Whiteside, 1981

Book publicists are in two businesses: books and show business.

➤ STUART APPELBAUM, publicity director, Bantam Books, quoted in *U.S. News & World Report,* December 5, 1983

In an industry where little money is spent on advertising, free publicity is the name of the game.

➤ "In Today's Marketplace, It's Hype, Hype, Hype," *U.S. News & World Report,* December 5, 1983

[Be] shameless. Try anything within reason to get your book noticed.

➤ WILLIAM TARG, advice to editors, "What's an Editor?," *Editors on Editing,* 1962

All publicity is good, except an obituary notice.

➤ BRENDAN BEHAN, Irish playwright/novelist, quoted in London *Sunday Express,* January 5, 1964

Silence equals death in our line of work.

➤ MARTIN J. SMITH, novelist, quoted in the *Los Angeles Times Magazine,* November 1, 1998

Some 42,000 books are published in the United States each year . . . The ratio of new books to those we have space to review is about 175 to one.

➤ Editorial, *The Nation,* November 20, 1982

When 500 books come across my desk, I have to discard ninetenths of them.

➤ REBECCA PEPPER SINKLER, former book editor of *The New York Times* and *Philadelphia Inquirer,* quoted in *Washington Journalism Review,* May 1983

One of the persistent scandals of American journalism is that so few papers are dedicated to the review of books.

➤ STEVE WASSERMAN, editor, *Los Angeles Times Book Review,* quoted in *Publishers Weekly,* July 7, 1997

Of the 50,000 or so books published in this country [last year], the [*Wall Street*] *Journal* reviewed about 210.

— DAVID BROOKS, *The Wall Street Journal*, December 1, 1988

No part of the Sunday paper has suffered more in the great space famine than the book section. To most editors—hardnosed, with a strong, hard news orientation—book coverage is at best an obligation to their intellectual readers and at least an anachronistic survival from the days when people actually read books. This is, after all, The Age of Television.

— BRUCE COOK, critic, *Washington Journalism Review*, May 1983

The *New York Times Book Review*, the *Los Angeles Times*'s "The Book Review," and the *Washington Post*'s "Book World" manage to give attention to a reasonable percentage of the 40,000 books that are published each year. "Reasonable" means between 3 and 5 percent (but don't try to convince an author whose book has been ignored by all three of the major book sections that the number is reasonable).

— BRUCE COOK, critic, *Washington Journalism Review*, May 1983

The real villains are media organizations unwilling to spend the money covering the book business that they spend on a lot of other things. Newspapers claim that they cover events, but thousands of events—the publication of general-interest books—are ignored each year by the same press that meticulously reports police blotter crimes of far less importance. Virtually every major movie, opera, TV show or sporting event is reviewed, but not every book.

— CARLIN ROMANO, book editor, *Philadelphia Inquirer,* quoted in *Publishers Weekly*, April 10, 1987

A book will not sell unless people know about it. The way most people know about things [today] is by watching their television sets, listening to the radio, and reading their newspapers.

— BOB GREENE, *Esquire*, March 1985

One would expect an industry that trumpets the public's right to know, the journalist's courageous quest for truth, to celebrate the book. The expectation is not fulfilled, partly because . . . newspaper editors fear and resent the greater thoroughness and sophistication of books.

　　―― CARLIN ROMANO, "Extra! Extra! The Sad Story of Books As News," essay in *Publishing Books* edited by Everette E. Dennis, Craig L. LaMay, and Edward C. Pease, 1997

[Radio] talk shows are the best sellers of books. I had James Michener on, and I asked him why he needed to do the show since he's one of the most popular novelists in America. And he said doing talk shows helped him sell 40 percent more books.

The reason is obvious: Listeners hear Michener and feel as if they have a personal relationship with him. When they go in the store and buy his book, they are buying someone they know.

　　―― LARRY KING, radio talk show host, quoted in *U.S. News & World Report,* January 16, 1984

I believe what makes books sell, more than anything else, is word of mouth.

　　―― NORA EPHRON, quoted in the *Boston Sunday Globe,* May 15, 1983

No matter how much you spend [on advertising], you can't buy that [word of mouth].

　　―― HOWARD KAMINSKY, former editor in chief, Random House, quoted in *The New York Times Book Review,* June 9, 1985

The best exposure, we all say, is word-of-mouth, but that is not the primary exposure. The primary exposure can be achieved in many ways: selection by a major book club, a super-hype publicity tour, or rave reviews in the major media. The trouble with all these ways is that they're generally all available to the same very few books.

　　―― GEORGE BROCKMAN, chairman, W. W. Norton & Co., paper presented at a seminar sponsored by the Center for the Book, April 25, 1980

The public buys best-sellers that are heavily advertised and publicized, just as they buy any product that is made highly visible.

➤ STANLEY J. CORWIN, *How to Become a Bestselling Author,* 1984

A new book is just like any new product, like a detergent. You have to acquaint people with it. They have to know it's there. You only get to be number one when the public knows about you.

➤ JACQUELINE SUSANN, novelist, quoted in *Lovely Me: The Life of Jacqueline Susann* by Barbara Seaman, 1987

Even if you have the next *Gone With the Wind,* it will not sell itself.

➤ BARBARA GRIER, vice president, Naiad Press, *Small Press,* November/December 1985

Some observers point to [Lee Iacocca's] best-selling book as evidence of his fame. But the book is just a byproduct of his being on TV. If Charlie the Tuna could write, he'd be on the best-seller lists.

➤ MIKE ROYKO, *Chicago Tribune,* February 20, 1986

Everybody sits back and prays for—gulp—good word of mouth. That's a funny way to run a business that's totally dependent on new products.

➤ COLIN L. JONES, "The Non Marketing of Fiction," *Publishers Weekly,* March 30, 1992

It's impossible to overpromote a book. In real estate, it's location, location, location. In book writing, it's promotion, promotion, promotion.

➤ ROBERT KOWALSKI, author, *The 8-Week Cholesterol Cure* (1989), speech before the Independent Writers of Southern California, January 28, 1991

If you have a book coming out, you have to get heavily—and intelligently—involved in marketing it or prepare to see it fail.

➤ JUDITH APPELBAUM, coauthor, *How to Get Happily Published,* interview in *Writers Write: The Internet Writing Journal,* June 1998

So many people think, "Well, there's the bookstore. I just got my book in there and I'm done. Everything else will be taken care of for me; I just go to my mailbox and pick up my check." That's the furthest thing from the truth.

    — JERROLD R. JENKINS, publishing consultant, quoted in Associated Press accounts, March 16, 1998

In today's market, writers can't just be writers. They have to be performers and publicists as well.

    — JOSHUA HENKIN, novelist, "Writer With a Roadshow," op-ed page article, *New York Times*, July 5, 1997

Don't expect anyone to do your selling for you. That's your job.

    — JOHN KREMER's warning to writers, *1,001 Ways to Market Your Books*, 1999

Publishers lavish promotion on books likely to sell, written by best-seller writers.

    — JEFF LIPPMAN, *The Wall Street Journal*, September 2, 1997

Everyone else pretty much has to fend for himself.

    — ROBERT CRAIS, author of the Elvis Cole mystery series, quoted in *The Wall Street Journal*, September 2, 1997

By the time each season's big books have been taken care of, there's precious little money or energy left for meritorious "mid-list" books, much less all that mediocrity.

    — JONATHAN YARDLEY, *Washington Post*, June 30, 1997

No matter how prestigious or enthusiastic your publisher is, your book probably won't be treated the way it should be. It's not that publishers don't want to support your books, or that they don't know how to generate sales; it's just that they don't have enough staff and money to give each book the attention it needs and deserves. As a result, most general-interest titles fizzle out fast. That's why smart authors get involved.

    — JUDITH APPELBAUM and FLORENCE JANOVIC, *The Writer's Workbook: A Full and Friendly Guide to Boosting Your Book's Sales*, 1991

I think the big myth in this business is that quality will win out, that cream will rise to the top. It's a misconception that I labored under when I was first getting into the business . . . What I learned is that the whole industry is driven by what I call The Big Push. Every publishing house sits down a few months prior to publication of its next list and makes a decision about which books get The Big Push. Very often, it's the books that they pay the most money for.
— RICK HORGAN, HarperCollins executive editor, in *Book Editors Talk to Writers* edited by Judy Mandell, 1995

Now the publicity challenge is to get "off-the-book-page" coverage. News stories, feature stories, *People* magazine interviews, and of course, Oprah. Increasingly, reviews . . . don't mean jack.
— MICHAEL WOLFF, "Is *The New York Times Book Review* Irrelevant?" *New York* magazine, October 12, 1998

In trade publishing, people read because publishing hype has made them want to read a book. Demand is created; thus the marketing of a trade book is in part the stimulation of interest rather than, as in scholarly publishing, the tapping of a pre-existing interest.
— IRVING LOUIS HOROWITZ, president, Transaction/Society, and Mary E. Curtis, editor in chief, Praeger Publishing, *The Nation*, June 3, 1978

No amount of promotion will sell a book that has no appeal.
— BERNARD GEIS, publisher, quoted in *Stranger Than Naked or How to Write Dirty Books for Fun and Profit* by Mike McGrady, 1970

Publicity will sell nothing unless people want it.
— WILLIAM PARKHURST, *How to Get Publicity*, 1985

Few nonfiction best-sellers were ever created or manufactured from remote subjects.
— STANLEY J. CORWIN, *How to Become a Bestselling Author*, 1984

It's impossible really to know what the public likes. The public's too fickle.
— Attributed to MALCOLM COWLEY, literary critic and historian

The only way to find out if a book is going to sell is to publish it.

— MICHAEL KORDA, *Another Life*, 1999

I've never quite bought the idea that the public buys or takes what it deserves. I think that . . . publishers to a measurable extent dictate public tastes. They're really more powerful than we want to admit.

— VAN ALLEN BRADLEY, literary critic, quoted in *Conversations* by Roy Newquist, 1967

I suspect that if any current product, be it an automobile, a vacuum cleaner, or whatever, were to be honestly described, there would be few takers. Books are no exceptions. You cannot permit them to come barefaced into being. They must be cosmetized, bewigged, perfumed, given padding where needed for the sake of appearance.

— DONALD MacCAMPBELL, *The Writing Business*, 1978

If you can't describe a book in one or two pithy sentences that would make you or my mother want to read it, then of course you can't sell it.

— MICHAEL KORDA, editor in chief, Simon & Schuster, quoted in *The Wall Street Journal*, June 26, 1984

Simon & Schuster runs a sales contest every year. The winners get to keep their jobs.

— JACK O'LEARY, former Simon & Schuster sales representative, half-joking about the company's approach to sales, *Newsweek*, July 24, 1984

One of the wonderful, sad and desperate things about this business is that nobody really knows how to sell books.

— ROGER STRAUS, III, publishing executive, quoted in *The Wall Street Journal*, August 2, 1990

It's a seat-of-the-pants, gut-instinct business. Our decisions aren't driven by market research.

— IRWYN APPLEBAUM, president and publisher, Bantam Books, quoted in *The Wall Street Journal*, January 10, 1997

Publishers and Publishing

The publishing industry functions as gatekeepers of ideas insofar as they make decisions about what to "let in" and what to "keep out."

⇥ LEWIS COSER, CHARLES KADUSHIN, and WALTER POWELL, *Books: The Culture and Commerce of Publishing,* 1982 (The authors note that "book reviewers, booksellers and literary agents can also be seen as gatekeepers.")

The largest floating crap game in the world.

⇥ Common publishing expression

In only rare cases do we know "for sure" what we have; almost all books perform above or below our expectations once they are published.

⇥ JAMES WADE and RICHARD MAREK, "Editing Nonfiction," *Editors on Editing* edited by Gerald Gross, 1962

Publishing has changed profoundly over the past 30 years. It has gone from being entrepreneurial, impresarial and academic to being run like a media business.

⇥ MORGAN ENTREKIN, Grove/Atlantic publisher, quoted in *Time,* April 6, 1998

Publishers have drastically changed the nature of what they published. The smaller books—serious fiction, art history, criticism—have all but disappeared from the lists of major houses.

⇥ ANDRÉ SCHIFFRIN, "The Corporatization of Publishing," *The Nation,* June 3, 1996

They want, not the book, understandably, but to balance the books.

⇥ MAUREEN HOWARD, "Before I Go, I Have Something to Say," *The New York Times Book Review,* April 25, 1982

Major commercial publishers essentially are giving up on literature . . . serious writing, whether poetry, essays and belles lettres,
more adventurous fiction (short and long) or thoughtful literary
criticism. The publishing of such work . . . is falling more and
more to smaller publishers all over the country.

> ← JOHN F. BAKER, summarizing the assessment of the head of the
> National Endowment of the Arts Literature Program, small
> publishers, writers, booksellers, literary consultants, and
> distributors, "Keeping Literature Alive," *Publishers Weekly*,
> December 12, 1986

Driven by dollar signs, many major publishers now reject most
manuscripts that don't instantly emit the sweet smell of success.

> ← MARK SOMMER, "Too Many Books, Too Few Serious Readers,"
> *Christian Science Monitor*, March 21, 1994

Since publication requires the investment of money, publishers
must be conned into doing good books.

> ← RICHARD KOSTELANETZ, *The End of Intelligent Writing*, 1974

I'm not saying all publishers have to be literary, but some interest
in books would help.

> ← A. N. WILSON, author, quoted in England's *Bookseller*,
> July 5, 1996

The notion that publishing was once a gentleman's game is as
much a fiction as anything [Edith Wharton or Sinclair Lewis] ever
wrote; publishing has always been about profits, literature second;
the main difference now being that it gives even less attention to
the latter than it did before.

> ← JONATHAN YARDLEY, *Washington Post*, June 30, 1997

There is a myth . . . about book publishing that it is a noble profession, an honorable and distinguished thing. The fact is, it's part of
the entertainment business.

> ← STEVEN SCHRAGIS, publisher, Carol Books, quoted in *New York*
> magazine, January 6, 1992

Publishing is an act of commerce. To stay in business, you must profit.

— RICHARD SNYDER, chairman, Simon & Schuster, quoted in *The New York Times Book Review,* December 9, 1979

The economics of publishing leave little leeway for putting out a Product that will not earn back its investment, let alone return a profit.

— JANE ADAMS, *How to Sell What You Write,* 1984

So long as publishing is an industry among industries, the prestige of whose executives depends on profits, it will wish to publish literature, especially very original literature, only as an expensive, if beloved hobby.

— ANNIE DILLARD, *Living by Fiction,* 1982

Every time we have to publish a public affairs book, we cringe. People forget about the event it deals with. The attention span of the American public is fleeting.

— ALBERTO VITALE, chairman and CEO of Random House, quoted in *The New Yorker,* October 6, 1997

I'm in the entertainment business, no doubt about it . . . The public has a voice, and its voice is heard by this industry. We may not like that voice; we might prefer that the public had different tastes. But my job is to responsibly entertain the public.

— PHYLLIS GRANN, chairperson, Putnam Berkeley Group, quoted in *Harper's,* August 1985

We sell books, other people sell shoes. What's the difference? Publishing isn't the highest art.

— MICHAEL KORDA, editor in chief, Simon & Schuster, quoted in *The New York Times Book Review,* December 9, 1979

Authors whose sales are slipping are likely to be let out to pasture.

— DONALD MAASS, *The Career Novelist,* 1996

I believe that we must realistically and frankly accept the book as a commodity, a product, an article of commerce . . . [A publisher's] products are products, like a piece of soap or a loaf of bread. As a matter of fact, we happen to offer food for the mind just as the grocer offers food for the body.

—— LEON SHIMKIN, retired publisher, Simon & Schuster, quoted in
Conversations by Roy Newquist, 1967

I think a lot of junk is published just because publishers think junk will sell.

—— VAN ALLEN BRADLEY, literary critic, quoted in *Conversations* by
Roy Newquist, 1967

We publish books because of their value as books . . . not simply because we think we can sell them. We believe if you give value, sales will follow.

—— CLAYTON CARLSON, vice president, Harper & Row, quoted in the
Newsletter on Intellectual Freedom, September 1983

It's a lot tougher world we are living in and we can't afford to take on the odd little book that tickles our fancy but will sell 900 to 1100 copies. We have to have reasons for doing a book other than our indulgences. We have to worry about making a profit so that we can continue to survive.

—— M. S. WYETH, another vice president at Harper & Row, quoted in
Publishers Weekly, August 15, 1980

Look, there are three or four reasons why you publish a book: for commercial reasons, because you think it will be a success; for artistic reasons, because it deserves to be published; as an investment in an author you hope will go on to greater things; and you can do a few purely at the whim of the publisher . . . You can no longer get by with sales of only 2500 to 3000 copies of a book; books that promise no more than that have got to come out.

—— NELSON DOUBLEDAY, president, Doubleday & Co., quoted in
Publishers Weekly, January 28, 1983

This may be a painful pill for would-be Faulkners and Austens to swallow, and my last desire is to denigrate the miraculous processes by which raw inspiration is transmuted into literature. But I do have to declare in all candor that no one interested in being published in our time can afford to be so naive as to believe a book will make it merely because it's good.

➤ RICHARD CURTIS, *How to Be Your Own Literary Agent,* 1983

I think what's going to happen is what happened in football—the smart agents are going to extract so much from the publishers that there won't be much left on the table (for other authors).

➤ MICHAEL THOMAS, novelist, quoted in Cleveland's *Plain Dealer,* September 23, 1985

We are going to eliminate the good, but less commercial book.

➤ JONI EVANS, then publisher, Linden Press, issuing a warning, quoted in *The New York Times Magazine,* May 21, 1978

The real victim in all this is the average book and the early efforts of promising writers—and this is a great, great sadness.

➤ Unidentified editor, quoted in *The New York Times Magazine,* May 21, 1978

Big corporations require big profits from big books, and the ones that tend to suffer are the offbeat, quirky, controversial or intellectually challenging ones.

➤ VIRGINIA BARBER, agent, quoted in *Publishers Weekly,* March 30, 1998

Big publishers will continue to do some serious books, assuming that their authors are media-promotable. That is really the key criterion these days in any publishing decision. The rest of them will go to university presses or they won't be published at all.

➤ ADAM BELLOW, editorial director, The Free Press, quoted in the *Chicago Tribune,* June 1, 1997

Trade publishers have, with few exceptions, summarily discarded serious authors with modest market potential. The books that remain . . . must run an increasingly punishing financial gauntlet.

— PHIL POCHODA, "Universities Press On," *The Nation,*
  December 23, 1997

It used to be that publishers would build writers book by book, slowly increasing sales. Now they want those authors to explode.

— MORGAN ENTREKIN, Grove/Atlantic publisher, quoted in the
  Los Angeles Times, November 13, 1997

Publishing is now saying that it's no longer going to subsidize a writer's development through a couple of books until the breakout one. It immediately wants a book that's commercial, that lunges forward.

— PETER J. SMITH, novelist, quoted in *Los Angeles* magazine,
  August 1997

In some companies editors have been told not to sign up anything that can't be counted on to hit at least 50,000 or some other arbitrary figure. Another command from on high is "buy only bestsellers."

— PAUL NATHAN, "The Golden Age of Opportunity," *Small Press,*
  September/October 1997

If I ran the publishing world, publishers would continue to support writers who are not, at this time, huge successes but who are developing well. I think that's the single most depressing aspect of the business these days—that writers are thrown aside far too soon, far too readily, far too callously and unwisely.

— DOMINICK ABEL, literary agent, quoted in *Speaking of Murder:
  Interviews with Masters of Mystery and Suspense* edited by Ed
  Gorman and Martin H. Greenberg, 1998

It's like show biz—you're only as good as your last book. The industry is becoming more like Hollywood, with all the pressure and focus on delivering blockbusters.

— FREDERICK R. LYNCH, author, quoted in *Investor's Business Daily,*
  May 29, 1998

It's very common for novelists to change their names and keep writing under different names until they have a bestseller. Because they are tracked by names in the computers of the bookstores . . . If you have a book that didn't move very well, your agent will say you have to change your name so that Crown Books or whatever chain can't tell you are the same person who only sold fifty thousand copies last time. Because they'd rather take a risk on a new writer than on one who has proven to be mid-level last time.

➤ CARLTON EASTLAKE, screenwriter, quoted in *The Screenwriting Life* by Rich Whiteside, 1998

New York publishing is self-destructing. They've forgotten what books are for. The only hope lies with the small presses that still care about ideas and authors, the craft of writing and the quality of books as cherished objects.

➤ An unidentified highly respected New York editor, quoted by Mark Sommer, "Too Many Books, Too Few Serious Readers," *Christian Science Monitor*, March 21, 1994

I think to a certain extent that a lot of the more adventurous writers—the good poets, writers of experimental fiction, and people with a lot of interesting, upbeat ideas—are giving up on mainstream publishers. They are signing on with the small houses because they think they will get a more sympathetic ear.

➤ JOHN F. BAKER, editor in chief, *Publishers Weekly*, speaking at a December 1982 symposium, "Trade Book Marketing in the 1980s"

The literary giants of tomorrow are probably being published by small presses today.

➤ KARIN TAYLOR, executive director, the Small Press Center, quoted in *The Writer*, April 1994

[Small presses] provide a great chance for the writer to write freely, without commercial restraint. They are just about the only place a new writer can get a hearing, the only place a writer can learn.

➤ BILL HENDERSON, publisher, Pushcart Press, quoted in *Wilson Library Bulletin*, November 1979

There are several advantages to working with a small publisher. One is that you have less in-house competition for editorial guidance and promotional efforts; if your work is successful, you're the big frog in the little pond. Small publishers are often willing to take risks that large houses would avoid; many of them set out avowedly to experiment.

➤ HAYES B. JACOBS, *Writer's Digest*, April 1985

The smaller operations count as great successes sales figures that would devastate a mainstream house. And they can lavish attention on a book that a conglomerate publisher would allow to languish rather than publish, marketing it expertly to the right audience.

➤ Editorial, "Is Publishing Perishing?" *The Nation*, March 17, 1997

With their large overheads, major publishers now have to do a minimum first run of 20,000–30,000 copies. For a smaller publisher, a title selling 5,000–10,000 copies is very profitable.

➤ DAN HALPERN, publisher of The Ecco Press, quoted in *Publishers Weekly*, June 15, 1998

A large commercial house has to plan on selling at least 15,000 copies of a book now to justify publishing it.

➤ MALCOLM JONES, JR., and RAY SAWHILL, "A Feast of Literary Delights," *Newsweek*, December 29, 1997–January 5, 1998

Authors should consider publishing with a smaller press if they are concerned about their book being lost on a massive list, of which only three or four command most of the publisher's attention; if their book is likely to reach a narrower-than-mass audience; if they prefer a nurturing, ongoing relationship with a publisher and editor; and if they want their book kept in print. Or if they want to be sure the book is published—edited, designed, produced and marketed—with care and enthusiasm along every step of the way.

➤ SCOTT WALKER, "Editing for a Small Press," in *Editors on Editing*, Third Edition, edited by Gerald Gross, 1985

In my opinion, independent houses have been the salvation of the serious literary book in America.
> ─ JACK SHOEMAKER, **editor in chief, North Point Press, quoted in** *Harper's*, **August 1985**

One of the liveliest cultural phenomena of our day.
> ─ NONA BALAKIAN, **referring to the emergence of small presses and magazines,** *Critical Encounters*, **1978**

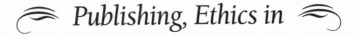

Publishing, Ethics in

It's interesting to think how . . . book publishing is so widely regarded as a business of great intellectual achievement—one of the last great gentlemanly businesses in the world. I've been at the bar for twenty-three years . . . Let me tell you, things have been pulled on me—in the gentlemanly publishing business— that are more venal than anything that was ever tried on me in Wall Street.
> ─ MORTON JANKLOW, **literary agent, quoted in** *The Blockbuster Complex* **by Thomas Whiteside, 1981**

I, too, have heard that publishing is a gentlemanly business, but it seems to me the gentlemanly gestures are expected mostly from the writers. All the rules go out the window as soon as money is involved.
> ─ CALVIN TRILLIN, *Uncivil Liberties*, **1982**

Publishers kill authors by creative bookkeeping . . . Publishers have always cheated authors . . . I believe that publishers are still cheating authors.
> ─ RICHARD CURTIS, *How to Be Your Own Literary Agent*, **1983**

The innocent writer can be eaten alive by a publisher's contract. It's common for publishers to try and take a share of movie rights, foreign rights, anything they can grab. Only an experienced agent knows when to make a canceling sweep of the pen.

➤ JOHN GARDNER, *On Becoming a Novelist,* 1983

Put two authors in a room and invariably they will begin trading tales of horror about how their publishers handled their books. In fact, it's the abundance of such stories that led *The New Yorker's* Calvin Trillin to threaten repeatedly (and only partly in jest) to compile "An Anthology of Authors' Atrocity Stories About Publishers." Perhaps, he's said, he'll even turn it into an annual. Clearly, there would be no shortage of contributors.

➤ REBEKAH JORDAN (pseudonym), "The Tangled Truth About Authors' Atrocity Stories," *Publishers Weekly,* May 21, 1979

Publishers are not necessarily either philanthropists or rogues . . . As a working hypothesis, regard them as ordinary human beings trying to earn their living at an unusually difficult occupation.

➤ SIR STANLEY UNWIN, perhaps countering Henry James's assertion that "Publishers are demons—there is no doubt about it," *The Truth About Publishing,* 1926

Not to generalize that it's a lousy business. But not to elevate it above the so-called commercial world, either.

➤ MORTON JANKLOW, literary agent, quoted in *The Blockbuster Complex* by Thomas Whiteside, 1981

You can hardly expect him to write his memoirs and say, "Yes, I'm a criminal." Simon & Schuster and I have always taken the position that if a book is interesting we should publish it. I don't think it's up to us to make a moral judgment.

➤ MICHAEL KORDA, editor in chief, Simon & Schuster, responding to criticisms that Joseph Bonnano's autobiography, *A Man of Honor* (1983), glorified or sanitized Bonnano's career in organized crime, quoted in *The New York Times,* June 3, 1983

We publish information. We can't control what people do with it.

— Rationale of Paladin publisher PETER LUND, who was sued for publishing a how-to murder manual, *Hitman* (1983), and *How to Make a Disposable Silencer* (1985) by relatives of a victim whose husband had hired a hit man to kill her, quoted in *Publishers Weekly*, May 19, 1997 (The convicted killer was found with the books in his possession. Police noted 22 instances in which the book's recommendations matched details of the murder.)

All the media are often guilty of producing outrageous trash and pretentious nonsense. But all of them have greatly enriched us as well on innumerable occasions. In particular, the book publishing industry, with all its faults, still constitutes a major civilizing force because books continue to respond to basic human needs and aspirations.

— JOHN DESSAUER, *Publishers Weekly*, November 26, 1978

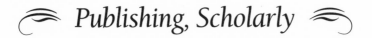

Publishing, Scholarly

They [university presses] were established because of the need to publish meritorious scholarly work that would not attract a large enough readership by commercial publishers.

— 1979 report of the American Council of Learned Societies

University-press publishing is rather analogous to public television. We have somewhat the same mission and we are both nonprofit.

— JOHN G. RYDEN, director, Yale University Press, quoted in *The New York Times*, April 20, 1984

Losing money is what university publishing is all about.

— Attributed to THOMAS MCFARLAND, director, University Press of New England

The university press is like the medieval monastery, lonely yeomen carrying the torch of learning. They publish what must be published, especially if they are books a commercial publisher wouldn't touch with a ten-foot salesman.

— GENE SHALIT, *Today* show critic, quoted in *Writer's Digest,* November 1978

Just one book, *Jaws,* has sold more copies than all of last year's university press books combined.

— GENE SHALIT, *Today* show critic, quoted in *Writer's Digest,* November 1978

If I had a book on the best seller list, I'd suspect I was doing something wrong.

— ARTHUR J. ROSENTHAL, former director, Harvard University Press, quoted in *The New York Times,* March 13, 1984 (However, later that year—in its 71st year of operation—Harvard University Press did have its first bestseller: Eudora Welty's autobiography, *One Writer's Beginnings.*)

Best-sellers are infrequent but not unknown in the world of university press publishing. There is a notion loose in the land that this is treason. Scholarly books are supposed to serve knowledge, not the marketplace; in academia it is often deemed better to perish than to be popular.

— HERBERT MITGANG, publishing correspondent, *The New York Times,* date unknown

We're allowed to make a profit, but over the long haul the red and black years tend to cancel out each other. It's like playing football against Princeton—you win one, you lose one. Our task is to break even.

— Attributed to CHESTER KERR, former director, Yale University Press

It has been timid editorially, conservative politically and esthetically.

— CHARLES NEWMAN, novelist and professor of literature, an indictment of university presses, *The Post-Modern Aura: The Art of Fiction in an Age of Inflation,* 1985

Mostly we have published for the smallest, narrowest constituency, the scholars in the sub-disciplines (not even the disciplines) and the libraries at the largest or richest universities.

— KENNETH ARNOLD, director, Rutgers University Press, "Taking Charge of the Future," *Scholarly Publishing,* January 1988

I think we are admirably filling the gap left by trade publishers, who are abandoning the kind of quality midlist fiction and nonfiction they used to do so well in the '70s and '80s. We're now doing many of the kinds of significant books on cultural and political issues that are part of the dialogue a civilized society requires.

— PHILIP POCHODA, editorial director, University Press of New England, quoted in *Publishers Weekly,* June 2, 1997

Mediocre manuscripts on routine, specialized topics—a category [Jane] Isay [former editor of Yale University Press] refers to as "15 Minutes With the French Revolution"—to be read routinely. They elicit no strong response one way or the other, and are therefore likely to be favorably reviewed.

Outstanding books, on the other hand, must meet high standards. Reviewers get provoked by such books, Ms. Isay said; they get interested and start to take issue with them—all of which tends to lead to a negative review.

She said she suspected that Plato, with his use of dialogue and his penchant for changing the subject, would have had a hard time with outside reviewers.

— *Chronicle of Higher Education,* reporting on a Wesleyan University conference on the scholarly publishing of controversial books, May 4, 1983

Quotes and Misquotes

The surest way to make a monkey of a man is to quote him.

— ROBERT BENCHLEY, *My Ten Years in a Quandary,* 1936

Next to being witty, the best thing is being able to quote another's wit.

➤ CHRISTOPHER N. BOVEE, writer, quoted in *Peter's Quotations* by Dr. Laurence J. Peter, 1977

I often quote myself. It adds spice to my conversation.

➤ GEORGE BERNARD SHAW, playwright, quoted in *Reader's Digest,* June 1943

Nothing gives an author so much pleasure as to find his works respectfully quoted by other learned authors.

➤ BENJAMIN FRANKLIN, *Poor Richard's Almanac,* 1738

Quotation is the highest compliment you can pay to an author.

➤ Attributed to SAMUEL JOHNSON, English writer, lexicographer, and critic

To be occasionally quoted is the only fame I hope for.

➤ ALEXANDER SMITH, *Dreamthorp,* 1863

The wisdom of the wise and the experience of the ages are perpetuated by quotations.

➤ ISAAC DISRAELI, *Curiosities of Literature,* 1793

It is a good thing . . . to read books of quotations . . . The quotations, when engraved upon the memory, give you good thoughts. They also make you anxious to read the authors and look for more.

➤ WINSTON CHURCHILL, *My Early Life: A Roving Commission,* 1958

I quote others only the better to express myself.

➤ MICHEL DE MONTAIGNE, *The Complete Essays of Montaigne* translated by Donald M. Frame, 1976

That was the reporter's fault. He should not have listened to me.

➤ Unknown

⟾ *Readers and Reading* ⟸

People say that life is the thing, but I prefer reading.
— LOGAN PEARSALL SMITH, *Afterthoughts,* 1931

Books are helpful in bed. But they are not responsive.
— MARY HEMINGWAY (Ernest's widow), quoted in *People,*
December 13, 1976

Perhaps the reason why the U.S.A. lags behind other nations in
book-reading is that there are so many people trying to write and
have no time left over for reading.
— *The Author and His Audience* by J. B. Lippincott Co., 1967

Almost nothing in our culture encourages the private moment of
reading.
— ELIZABETH SIFTON, editor, Viking Penguin, quoted in *Harper's,*
August 1985

Of all the many things in which we recognize some universal comfort—God, sex, food, family, friends—reading seems to be the one
in which the comfort is most undersung, at least publicly.
— ANNA QUINDLEN, *How Reading Changed My Life,* 1998

While we pay lip service to the virtues of reading, the truth is that
there is still in our culture something that suspects those who read
too much, whatever reading too much means, of being lazy, aimless
dreamers, people who need to grow up and come outside to where
real life is, who think themselves superior in their separateness.
— ANNA QUINDLEN, *How Reading Changed My Life,* 1998

There can be no such thing, really, as too many books, only too few
readers.
— Editorial, *The Nation,* November 20, 1982

As kids, we found books and reading instruments of torture rather than pleasure and enhancement. There's a psychological obstacle that has to be overcome so more people will realize it's ten times more fun to read a book than to watch *Columbo.*

— ROGER STRAUS, III, publishing executive, quoted in *Publishers Weekly,* July 7, 1973

Booksellers and publishers of books are feeling the results of mass illiteracy . . . Twenty-seven percent of adults under twenty-one do not read books at all.

— JONATHAN KOZOL, *Illiterate America,* 1985

Every man who knows how to read has it in his power to magnify himself, to multiply the ways which he exists, to make his life full, significant and interesting.

— Attributed to ALDOUS HUXLEY, **English novelist**

Reading maketh a full man.

— FRANCIS BACON, *Essays, Civil, and Moral,* 1909

I divide all readers into two classes: those who read to remember and those who read to forget.

— WILLIAM LYON PHELPS, educator and critic, quoted in *Reader's Digest,* December 1940

Rejection

Remember, an editor is not God, only a person with a certain viewpoint, certain taste; therefore, don't let rejection stop you from writing or sending out.

— TOI DERRICOTE, poet, quoted in *The First-Book Market* edited by Jason Shinder, 1998

Personally, I don't mind if a publisher rejects my work. It's when they return it by "junk mail."
  — ROBERT ORBEN, *The Encyclopedia of One-Liner Comedy,* 1971

A rejection (which in any case is directed toward your work and not to you as a person) may well reflect more unfavorably on the editor's ability than on yours.
  — JUDITH APPELBAUM and NANCY EVANS, *How to Get Happily Published,* 1976

I think the percentage of very good books—the really notable books—that are declined is higher than the percentage of highly competent mediocrities. The reason is that the books of the greatest talent are almost always full of trouble, and difficult, and they do not conform to the usual standards.
  — MAXWELL E. PERKINS, editor, letter to Alice D. Bond, July 17, 1944, quoted in *Editor to Author: The Letters of Maxwell E. Perkins* selected and edited by John Hall Wheelock, 1950

Mame garnered something like 52 rejections before it was sold. The number of books that become hits after being rejected is enormous. The reason is, really good work is *different,* and different means risk to an editor.
  — JAMES N. FREY, "The Mother of All Attitudes," in *The Portable Writers' Conference* edited by Stephen Blake Mettee, 1997

The history of publishing is replete with tales of editorial idiocy.
  — Unidentified editor, "How Book Publishing Decisions Are Made," *1983 Writer's Handbook*

John Gardner wrote four complete novels . . . before he sold one. John Grisham's first novel, *A Time to Kill,* was rejected 25 times. William Faulkner's first few novels sold only about 2,000 copies each, in their initial printings. Dr. Seuss was told by an editor that saw his first book, *And to Think That I Saw It on Mulberry Street,* was "too different from other juveniles on the market to warrant its selling."
  — NANCY KRESS, *Writer's Digest,* October 1993

Who wants to read about bums, and especially bums in Albany?

➤ What William Kennedy was repeatedly told when he tried to sell his novel *Ironweed,* a book that was rejected 13 times before winning a 1984 National Book Critics Circle award and the 1984 Pulitzer Prize for fiction, quoted in *The New York Times Book Review,* April 8, 1984

No one would want to read about a presidential campaign after it was finished.

➤ What Theodore White was told before embarking on his very successful *Making of the President* series, quoted in *The New York Times Book Review,* May 6, 1984

Has no reader interest.

➤ A British publisher rejecting Frederick Forsyth's *Day of the Jackal,* a novel that subsequently sold 8 million copies, quoted in *The Experts Speak* by Christopher Cerf and Victor Navasky, 1984

Who in hell wants to read about a bunch of crazy Scandinavians floating around the ocean in a raft?

➤ A publisher who turned down Thor Heyerdahl's *Kon-Tiki* (1950), a book that topped *The New York Times* best-seller list for over a year, quoted in *The Experts Speak* by Christopher Cerf and Victor Navasky, 1984

Look, they're not interested in a talking seagull.

➤ What Richard Bach's agent told him after his novel *Jonathan Livingston Seagull* (1970) was rejected more than 20 times. The book went on to sell 3,107,500 copies in hardback. The only novel to ever sell more hardcover copies is Margaret Mitchell's *Gone With the Wind. The New York Times Book Review,* July 21, 1985

A period novel! About the Civil War! Who needs the Civil War now—who cares?

➤ HERBERT R. MAYES, editor, *Pictoral Review,* turning down the opportunity to serialize Margaret Mitchell's *Gone With the Wind* (1936), quoted in *The Magazine Maze* by Herbert R. Mayes, 1980

Face it . . . "Parables don't sell."

— What Jack Canfield and Mark Victor Hansen's agent told them after their 33d rejection. [Their book, *Chicken Soup for the Soul* (1993), was formally rejected over 100 times—and informally another 111 times at an American Booksellers Association convention—before a small Florida publisher agreed to take it on. *Chicken Soup for the Soul* went on to sell 7 million copies. It also spawned numerous sequels that sold another 28 million books.] Quoted in *Time*, June 8, 1998

Not one expert in the magazine business thought there was (a market for *Ms*)—not one.

— GLORIA STEINEM, founder, *Ms* magazine

If it hadn't been for a tiny, independent, nonprofit press in upstate New York, the 1985 Pulitzer Prize-winner in poetry might never have been published: Carolyn Kizer's *Yin* had been rejected by several large commercial houses.

— *Publishers Weekly*, May 10, 1985

To see what chance a talented, unknown author had of getting a novel published or represented, I typed up Jerzy Kosinski's *Steps* and submitted it, untitled, to 14 major publishing houses and 13 literary agents. To another 13 agents a letter of inquiry was sent. (The highly acclaimed novel won the National Book Award for Fiction in 1969.)

The book was rejected by all 14 publishing houses (including Random House, the original publisher of *Steps*) and the 26 agents. None recognized the work, and no one thought it deserved to be published.

— CHUCK ROSS, *Chicago Sun-Times*, March 30, 1980

A southern writer named John Kennedy Toole wrote a comic novel about life in New Orleans called *A Confederacy of Dunces*. It was so relentlessly rejected by publishers that he killed himself. That was in 1969. His mother refused to give up on the book. She sent it out and got it back, rejected, over and over again. At last she won the patronage of Walker Percy, who got it accepted by the Louisiana State University Press, and in 1980 it won a Pulitzer Prize for fiction.

— JOHN WHITE, *Rejection*, 1982

William Saroyan was one of the most published writers in American letters. He worked in nearly every literary genre and has had tremendous success in each. I'm told that when he started writing and sending manuscripts, he began the practice of putting the rejection slips in a stack beside his desk. When he had his first acceptance, the stack of rejection slips was even with the top of his desk.

— LEE PENNINGTON, *Writer's Digest,* August 1982

Lee Pennington has been published in more than 300 magazines— and rejected so many thousand times that in one six-month period he papered all four walls of a room with rejection slips.

— JOHN WHITE, *Rejection,* 1982

I've filled scrapbooks with them [rejection slips] . . . I use rejection slips as coasters . . . Sometimes I have rejection parties.

— LEE PENNINGTON, *Writer's Digest,* August 1982

Here is his record for failure. From the time John Toland started writing for publication he produced six novels. None was published. He wrote twenty-five completed plays. None was produced. He wrote more than one hundred short stories before one was published. John Toland was forty-two years old before his first book was published. It was not until after twenty years of diligent writing and rewriting that he stumbled upon, or had thrust upon him, the one discovery that enabled him to become a success as an author of books.

— RALPH DAIGH, *Maybe You Should Write a Book,* 1977

I've always had complete confidence in myself. When I was nothing, I had complete confidence. There were ten guys in my writing class at Williams College who could write better than I. They didn't have what I have, which is guts. I was dedicated to writing and nothing could stop me.

— JOHN TOLAND, author, quoted in *Writer's Digest,* April 1978

If every [literary] agent in the end turns you down, you know you're either not good enough or too good. If you're too good, keep writing, and keep your contacts with the writing community available to you, and eventually your day will come.

—JOHN GARDNER, *On Becoming a Novelist*, 1983

What did you think? That I was going to let myself be stopped by a couple hundred idiot publishers?

—WILLIAM A. GORDON, explaining why he relentlessly submitted his book, *Four Dead in Ohio* (1995), reappraising the 1970 Kent State shootings. The book, which was eventually published by Prometheus Books after nine years of submissions, was praised by *Choice* magazine, which described it "as entertaining as the best detective fiction and as analytical and well documented as the best journalism or scholarship." (In other comments, Gordon, now a full-time author and publisher, said: "They're going to be talking about that book as long as books are published.")

Any ambitious would-be author worth half his salt would prefer notoriety to neglect.

—SCOTT RICE, English professor, San Jose State University, Introduction to *It Was a Dark and Stormy Night*, 1984

Bill's big success is based on failure.

—Headline of an Australian newspaper, November 11, 1975, describing the efforts of Bill Gold, the author of an unpublished novel about the publishing game, *One Best Seller*. Gold reaped extraordinary publicity for his efforts; however, he was not able to capitalize on his opportunity because he did not have a salable product.

(For additional related quotes, see also *Success and Failure*)

⌇ *Research and Scholarship* ⌇

Facts do not cease to exist because they are ignored.
➤ ALDOUS HUXLEY, *Proper Studies*, 1927

Get your facts first, and then you can distort 'em as much as you please.
➤ MARK TWAIN, novelist, quoted in *From Sea to Sea* by Rudyard Kipling, 1900

To treat your facts with imagination is one thing, but to imagine your facts is another.
➤ JOHN BURROUGHS, essayist, quoted in *Peter's Quotations* by Dr. Laurence J. Peter, 1977

Faulty research is like a faulty septic tank. Sooner or later the evidence will surface and become embarrassing.
➤ REX ALLEN SMITH, writer, quoted in *The Self-Publishing Manual* by Dan Poynter, 1999

Research is absolutely essential for me. The trick is to know when to finally stop doing it and actually go to work.
➤ LARRY GELBART, *Laughing Matters*, 1998

A man will turn over half a library to make one book.
➤ SAMUEL JOHNSON, English writer, lexicographer, and critic, quoted in *Life of Johnson* by James Boswell, 1791

The next scholar sucks the few drops of honey that you have accumulated, sets right your blunders, and you are superseded.
➤ A. C. BENSON, *From a College Window*, 1906

In the spider-web of facts, many a truth is strangled.
➤ PAUL ELDRIDGE, *Horns of Glass*, 1943

The most important things are not always to be found in the files.

➤ JOHANN WOLFGANG VON GOETHE, *Maxims and Reflections of Goethe*, 1893

The memorandum is written to protect the writer—not to inform his readers.

➤ DEAN ACHESON, former U.S. secretary of state, quoted in *The Wall Street Journal*, September 8, 1977

Do not become archivists of facts. Try to penetrate to the secret of their occurrence, persistently search for the laws which govern them.

➤ IVAN PAVLOV, Russian physiologist, "To the Academic Youth of Russia," February 27, 1936

The ultimate goal of all research is not objectivity, but truth.

➤ HELENE DEUTSCH, psychiatrist, Preface to *The Psychology of Women*, 1944

A deluge of words and a drop of sense.

➤ DR. THOMAS FULLER, *Gnomolgia*, 1732

It is a safe rule to apply that, when a mathematical or philosophical author writes with a misty profundity, he is talking nonsense.

➤ Attributed to ALFRED NORTH WHITEHEAD, English mathematician and philosopher

Professors are often shy, timid and even fearful people, and . . . dull, difficult prose can function as kind of a protective camouflage. When you write typical academic prose, it is nearly impossible to make a strong, clear statement. The benefit here is that no one can attack your position, say you are wrong or even raise questions about the accuracy of what you have said, if they cannot tell what you have said. In those terms, awful, indecipherable prose is its own form of armor, protecting the fragile, sensitive thoughts of timid souls.

➤ PATRICIA NELSON LIMERICK, "The Trouble With Academic Prose," *Current*, February 1994

The vast majority of the so-called research turned out in the modern university is essentially worthless. It does not result in any measurable benefit to anything or anybody. It does not push back those omnipresent "frontiers of knowledge" so confidently evoked; it does not in the main result in greater health or happiness among the general populace or any particular segment of it. It is busywork on a vast, incomprehensible scale.

— PAGE SMITH, *Killing the Spirit: Higher Education in America,* 1990

[Academic research] falsifies human experience and the true nature of research. If bad research (not technically "bad" or methodologically bad but unimportant and largely irrelevant research) does not drive out good, it constantly threatens to bury the good in a vast pile of mediocrity. It encourages the notion, moreover, that routine, pedestrian work has some useful function in God's plan for the universe.

— PAGE SMITH, *Killing the Spirit: Higher Education in America,* 1990

By its very nature, scholarly prose lacks the rhetorical virtue of reckless passion. Custom and propriety hem the scholar in on every side.

— MARY-CLAIRE VAN LEUNEN, *A Handbook for Scholars,* 1977

I believe that the lies told by important men—Churchill, Haldeman, Nixon—should be published; they are part of the record from which the truth will be distilled now and in the future.

— PETER PRESCOTT, *Newsweek* critic, writing in *The Nation,*
   June 3, 1978

It often happens that, if a lie be believed only for an hour, it has done its work.

— THOMAS SWIFT, editor, *The Examiner,* circa 1713

A lie can travel half way around the world before Truth puts its boots on.

— Variously attributed

Few nonfiction books are checked for accuracy. As a result inaccuracies abound ... Many consumers are aware that the *National Enquirer* is an unreliable newspaper, but they have no idea which book publishers are the industry's *National Enquirer* equivalents.

— Steve Weinberg, referring to publishing's dirty secret, *Columbia Journalism Review,* August 1991

Books are written and published every day making claims that are subsequently proven to be untrue, or biased, or partially true. The competitive and corrective process of a free society provides its own corrective.

— Townsend Hoopes, president, Association of American Publishers, responding to criticisms about the publication of David Rorvik's book *In His Image,* 1978 (The book claimed—without proof—that a man had been cloned, and subsequently came under severe attack by the scientific community.)

Scholars do not always read the scientific literature carefully. Science is not a perfectly objective process. Dogma and prejudice, when suitably garbled, creep into science just as easily as into any other human enterprise, and maybe more easily since their entry is unexpected.

— William Broad and Nicholas Wade, *Betrayers of the Truth: Fraud and Deceit in the Halls of Science,* 1982

When scholarship is at its worst, we create new myths out of our memories; when it is at its best, we recover a part of the lost or forgotten.

— Lester A. Beaurline, *A Mirror for Modern Scholars,* 1966

 *Revisions*

Too much polishing weakens rather than improves a work.

— Pliny the Younger, Roman governor, *Letters and Panegyricus,* 1969

A good [publishing] house should be able to recognize a publishable work even in rougher form, but many cannot.

➤ CHUCK ROSS, *Chicago Sun-Times,* March 30, 1982

If it isn't good enough when we first see it, it doesn't get published.

➤ Attributed to FREDERICK PRAEGER, president, Praeger Publishers, summarizing the attitude of many publishers

An author's first draft is often remarkably dissimilar from the finished product, and even the reworked manuscript an author submits to a publisher bears only passing resemblance to what finally appears between the covers.

➤ EDWIN MCDOWELL, publishing correspondent, *The New York Times,* December 1982

The majority of published writers I have known write first drafts that are riddled with craft errors and embarrassingly bad writing compared to the version that finally sees print. They know that writing is truly rewriting.

➤ SOL STEIN, *Stein on Writing,* 1995

A professional writer is a professional reviser.

➤ JOHN LONG, *Writer's Little Book of Wisdom,* 1996

First drafts are for learning what your novel or story is about. Revision is working with that knowledge to enlarge or enhance an idea, or reform it.

➤ BERNARD MALAMUD, novelist, quoted in *First Person Singular* compiled by Joyce Carol Oates, 1983

Nothing comes out right the first time. A first draft is an outline, nothing more.

➤ JAMES W. BLINN, novelist, quoted in *The Writer,* July 1997

I can't write five words but that I change seven.

➤ DOROTHY PARKER, humorist, quoted in *The Paris Review,* Spring 1956

Every single [writer] I know writes really awful first drafts, and these are people who write books that sell millions of copies.

— ANNE LAMOTT, author of *Bird By Bird: Some Instructions on Writing and Life,* interviewed on *The Best of NPR: Writers on Writing* (National Public Radio audiobook), 1994

The best authors are always the severest critics of their own works; they revise, correct, file and polish them, till they think they have brought them to perfection.

— EARL OF CHESTERFIELD, English politician and letter writer in a letter to his son Philip Stanhope, May 6, 1751

The biggest difference between a writer and a would-be writer is their attitude toward rewriting . . . Unwillingness to revise usually signals an amateur.

— SOL STEIN, *Stein on Writing,* 1995

There are very few pages in *Ragtime* that I didn't write a half-dozen times or more.

— E. L. DOCTOROW, novelist, quoted in *Conversations With American Writers* by Charles Ruas, 1985

I've done as many as eighty drafts of one poem . . . I've found students shocked to learn that it can take me three years to finish a poem.

— CAROLYN FORCHE, poet, quoted in *The Writing Business: A Poets & Writers Handbook,* 1985

I rewrite everything, almost idiotically. I rewrite and work and work, and rewrite and rewrite some more.

— LAURA Z. HOBSON, novelist, quoted in *Conversations* by Roy Newquist, 1967

I rewrote the ending to *Farewell to Arms,* the last page of it, thirty-nine times before I was satisfied.

— ERNEST HEMINGWAY, novelist, quoted in *The Paris Review,* Spring 1958

[Margaret Mitchell] said she had written at least forty first chapters . . . and that whenever she had nothing to do and nothing to read, she had written another first chapter and each one looked worse than the last.

━ ANNE EDWARDS, *The Road to Tara,* 1983

I work over my manuscript many times until I feel there is nothing more than I can change to improve it.

━ Attributed to SAUL BELLOW, novelist

Revision is almost always necessary. A book is never "finished" or "perfect."

━ SHANNON RAVENEL, editorial director, Algonquin Books of Chapel Hill, quoted in *Writer's Digest,* October 1994

There are passages in every novel whose first writing is pretty much the last. But it's the joint and cement, between those spontaneous passages, that takes a great deal of rewriting.

━ THORNTON WILDER, playwright and novelist, quoted in *The Paris Review,* Winter/Spring 1957

If it doesn't work, begin something else.

━ BERNARD MALAMUD, novelist, quoted in *Words and Their Masters* by Israel Shenker, 1974

The wastepaper basket is still the writer's best friend.

━ ISAAC BASHEVIS SINGER, short-story writer/novelist, quoted in *The Book of Quotes* by Barbara Rowes, 1979

A really great novel is made with a knife and not a pen. A novelist must have the intestinal fortitude to cut out even the most brilliant passage so long as it doesn't advance the story.

━ Attributed to FRANK YERBY, novelist

Don't try to save junk just because it took you a long time to write it.

━ DAVID EDDINGS, writer, quoted in *Writer's Digest,* August 1994

A thing may in itself be the finest piece of writing one has ever done, and yet have absolutely no place in the manuscript one hopes to publish.

➤ Attributed to THOMAS WOLFE, novelist

A successful book is not made of what is in it, but what is left out of it.

➤ MARK TWAIN, novelist, letter to William Dean Howells, February 23, 1897, quoted in *Mark My Words* by Mark Dawidziak, 1996

I know it's finished when I can no longer stand working on it.

➤ BERNARD MALAMUD, novelist, quoted in *Words and Their Masters* by Israel Shenker, 1974

A writer knows when his book is finished, in the same way that an artist knows when his painting is finished.

➤ SIDNEY SHELDON, "Speaking of Fiction," *1995 Writer's Handbook*

You should have seen the first draft!

➤ An editor's typical excuse after a book reviewer criticizes a book for either being poorly written or poorly edited

Satire

The job of satire is to frighten and enlighten.

➤ Attributed to RICHARD CONDON, novelist

The goal of Satire is reform, the goal of Comedy acceptance.

➤ Attributed to W. H. AUDEN, poet and playwright

To be comic is merely to be playful, but wit is a serious matter.

➤ AMBROSE BIERCE, 1903 essay, "Wit and Humor"

Satire [is] a form of writing in which the message is serious and the method is humor.

➤ DR. LAURENCE J. PETER, *Why Things Go Wrong or the Peter Principle Revisited,* 1985

I think satire is among the most powerful weapons we have. You can do more with it than any other kind of writing.

➤ ART BUCHWALD, interview, *Playboy,* April 1965

I'd say roughly that the difference between a satirist and a humorist is that the satirist shoots to kill while the humorist brings his prey back alive.

➤ PETER DE VRIES, novelist, quoted in *Counterpoint* compiled and edited by Roy Newquist, 1964

An ounce of ridicule is often more potent than a hundred-weight of argument.

➤ ANTHONY TROLLOPE, *The Eustace Diamonds,* 1872

A man can't write successful satire except he be in a calm judicial good humor . . . I don't ever seem to be in a good enough humor with anything to satirize it. No, I want to stand up before it and curse it and foam at the mouth—or take a club and pound it to rags and pulp.

➤ MARK TWAIN, novelist, letter to William Dean Howells, January 30, 1879, quoted in *The Selected Letters of Mark Twain* edited by Charles Neider, 1982

Only exceptionally rational men can afford to be absurd.

➤ ALLAN GOLDFEIN, writer, quoted in *Peter's Quotations* by Dr. Laurence J. Peter, 1976

Satire requires a nimble mind, the ability to make leaps of the imagination. One must have a profound knowledge of a subject to satirize it, since it must be carried beyond its normal form and then distorted in order to show its various facets.

➤ JOHN BAILEY, *Intent on Laughter,* 1976

Before one can satirize a subject effectively he must know pretty much all there is to know about it. Satire is more intellectual than other types of humor. It demands a good deal of the reader. What's more, it has a purpose other than to make you laugh, and that is to point out a fault or foible, to deflate pomposity.

> ━ RICHARD ARMOUR, satirist, quoted in *I Get My Best Ideas in Bed: And Other Words of Wisdom From 190 of America's Best-Selling Authors* edited by William Melton, 1971

Satire is not the greatest type of literature . . . Still, it is one of the most original, challenging and memorable forms.

> ━ GILBERT HIGHET, *The Anatomy of Satire,* 1962

Men have written satire on the gravest of themes and the most trivial, the most austere and the most licentious, the most sacred and the most profane, the most delicate and the most disgusting. There are few topics which satirists cannot handle.

> ━ GILBERT HIGHET, *The Anatomy of Satire,* 1962

When a satirist uses uncompromisingly clear language to describe unpleasant facts and people, he intends to do more than make a statement. He intends to shock his readers.

> ━ GILBERT HIGHET, *The Anatomy of Satire,* 1962

Though laughter is his mode, the satirist is . . . fundamentally a moralist.

> ━ MARTIN C. BATTESTIN, Introduction to *Joseph Andrews/Shamela* by Henry Fielding, 1972

Great satire has always had some sort of moral underpinnings.

> ━ GARRY TRUDEAU, *The People's Doonesbury,* 1981

Satire is moral outrage transformed into comic art.

> ━ PHILIP ROTH, *Reading Myself and Others,* 1975

In America, the only political satirists left are the cartoonists. Everyone else is vying for a good table at the White House Correspondents' Dinner.

➤ JAMES ATLAS, "A Vituperative Art," *The New Yorker,*
June 15, 1998

Satirists are not supposed to be balanced. They're supposed to be unfair . . . It's part of the job description.

➤ GARRY TRUDEAU, creator, "Doonesbury," speech at an Associated Press Managing Editors convention, November 27, 1984

There is no denying that satire is an ungentlemanly art.

➤ GARRY TRUDEAU, speech, "What a Long Strange Strip It's Been," quoted in the Los Angeles *Daily News,* June 30, 1997

It's the world that's gone nuts, not me. It's the world that's turned into a satire.

➤ PADDY CHAFEVSKY, novelist and screenwriter of *Network,* quoted in *The Craft of the Screenwriter* by John Brady, 1981

One *Catch-22* or *Dr. Strangelove* is more powerful than all the books and movies that try to show war "as it is" . . . One cartoon by Herblock or by Bill Mauldin is worth a hundred solemn editorials.

➤ WILLIAM ZINSSER, *On Writing Well,* 1976

The program you are about to see is "All in the Family." It seeks to throw a humorous spotlight on our frailties, prejudices and concerns. By making them a source of laughter, we hope to show—in a mature fashion—just how absurd they are.

➤ Announcer describing the television program to a preview audience, January 21, 1971

Satire is what closes on Saturday night.

➤ GEORGE S. KAUFMAN, playwright, quoted in *George S. Kaufman* by Howard Teichmann, 1972

Creatures like George S. Kaufman . . . don't even know what satire is . . . Their stuff is as dull as yesterday's newspaper. Successful satire has got to be pretty good the day after tomorrow.

— DOROTHY PARKER, humorist, quoted in *The Paris Review,* Spring 1956

(For additional related quotes, see also *Wit*)

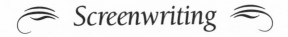 *Screenwriting*

The most important element in any movie is the screenwriter, his story and his words.

— LIZ SMITH, gossip columnist, *New York Post,* May 7, 1996

It starts with what's on the page. To me the biggest star of any page is what's on the page—in other words, the writer. I don't care how many actors or stars are in the picture, or who's directing it or who's producing it or what company's releasing it—if it isn't on the page, it's not going to work. That's your biggest star—the writer.

— ROBERT EVANS, producer, quoted in *The Culture Barons* by Faye Levine, 1976

Everyone knows that the screenplay is never the decisive factor [in deciding whether a movie is filmed]. What counts is the deal structure, where something is shot, what stars are lined up.

— JIM HARRISON, novelist and screenwriter, quoted in *Time* magazine, September 2, 1985. Harrison, who has had 19 books of fiction, poetry, and prose published, and whose screenwriting credits include *Wolf* (1994) and *Revenge* (1990), wrote and sold 15 screenplays before one was actually produced.

Film is a director's medium . . . A number of us have written prose fiction for many years and won awards which are perceived as external signs of success. But to think that we can sit down and write a play or a movie is a complete mistake . . . It's like the difference between jogging and swimming. You have to use a whole different set of muscles, beginning again—virtually at zero.

— JOYCE CAROL OATES, novelist, quoted in the *Los Angeles Times,* May 9, 1991

Believe me, if you can think of a good script, they'll grab it. There aren't too many good scripts around.

— Attributed to PADDY CHAFEVSKY, screenwriter and novelist

There are only eleven good writers in all of Hollywood.

— MEL BROOKS, filmmaker, quoted in *The Craft of the Screenwriter* by John Brady, 1981

Film is the only way to reach out to people all over the world. The time of the book is over.

— Attributed to COSTA-GAVRAS, director

The movies are the new literature.

— CECIL B. DEMILLE, director, quoted in *Cecil B. DeMille* by Charles Higham, 1973

When you think about it, who has more power to influence people than filmmakers?

— WOLF SCHNEIDER, *American Film,* May 1991

The truth is this: The power of a movie tends to last only as long as the lights are down and the screen flickers. While you're watching it, it owns you. But as soon as you walk out of the theater and the cold air hits your face, the movie starts to evaporate, almost like it's leaking through your skin. By the time you reach the parking lot, it's mostly gone.

— ROBERT A. JONES, *Los Angeles Times,* January 12, 1992

We sometimes do screenplays by committee.

> ← WILLIAM PETER BLATTY, novelist and screenwriter, quoted in
> *Counterpoint* compiled and edited by Roy Newquist, 1964

It's a bastard art . . . in that no one reads what you write, except
people who are going to destroy it.

> ← Attributed to DAVID GILLER, screenwriter

A novelist, a singer, a sculpturer—they can just do it and it's done.
I know that's a might simplification, but when a screenwriter "does
it," it's not done—it's just begun. No one has to go through an
uglier, middleman-packed, Chinese telephone torture than a
screenwriter does.

> ← DANIEL WATERS, screenwriter, writing in *Why We Write* edited by
> Lorian Tamara Elbert, 1999

Since the copyright does not belong to the writer, a powerful producer, director, or actor can take the raw material already sausaged
by the studio bureaucracy and submit it to his wife, chauffeur,
mistress, agent or talented nephew for further "improvement."

> ← JOHN BRILEY, screenwriter, writing in *Why We Write* edited by
> Lorian Tamara Elbert, 1999

Finish a book and there is a sense of accomplishment; finish a
script and the shit starts.

> ← Attributed to JOHN GREGORY DUNNE, novelist and screenwriter

I'm pretty bad about deviating from the words on the page because
I only view a script as a blueprint. It's written to be revised. The
process is that you're making a movie, not photographing a
screenplay. The screenplay is simply one of the tools you use to get
there.

> ← JOHN MCTIERNAN, action director, whose credits include *Die
> Hard, Die Hard With a Vengeance, Predator,* and *Last Action Hero,*
> quoted in *The Insider's Guide to Writing for Screen and Television*
> by Ronald B. Tobias, 1997

So often you hear the uniformed response: "The screenplay is just the blueprint for a film." But how many buildings turn out well with a bad set of blueprints? Or more importantly: Who's more crucial to the job, your architect or your contractor?

> ⟶ GARY ROSS, screenwriter/director, writing in *Why We Write* edited by Lorian Tamara Elbert, 1999

In Hollywood, the writer is regarded as someone you can buy and replace.

> ⟶ STIRLING SILLIPHANT, screenwriter, quoted in *Reel Power* by Mark Litwak, 1996

There are fewer stars for writers on the Hollywood Walk of Fame than there are for animals.

> ⟶ ALJEAN HARMETZ, *The New York Times*, July 8, 1990

They ruin your stories. They massacre your ideas. They prostitute your art. They trample on your pride. And what do you get for it? A fortune.

> ⟶ Unidentified screenwriter, quoted in *Saturday Review,* December 26, 1970

If you are lucky or talented enough to become in demand as a screenwriter, the amounts you are paid are so staggering, compared to real writing, that it's bound to make you uneasy.

> ⟶ WILLIAM GOLDMAN, *Adventures in the Screen Trade,* 1983

Pity the poor—or even the rich—Hollywood screenwriter. Unlike his compatriot novelists, playwrights, journalists or even poets, nobody knows his name. Or cares.

> ⟶ MARCIA SELIGSON, *The New York Times Magazine,* July 19, 1970

I tried to keep that larcenous, cynical view as much as I could, because I thought that's what it would take to get me through, and it worked.

> ⟶ SCOTT SPENCER, novelist, quoted in *Conversations With American Writers* by Charles Ruas, 1985

Writing a good movie brings a writer about as much fame as riding a bicycle.

— Attributed to BEN HECHT, screenwriter

The writers who feel a lot of pride cannot survive here. They are better suited to writing books and plays where they can retain control.

— JAREM LARDNER, screenwriter, quoted in *Reel Power* by Mark Litwak, 1986

People who run down screenplays because they don't like the form is a little like saying, "You make very beautiful chairs, but I can't take them seriously because all they do is hold people's butts up."

— Attributed to THOMAS McGUANE, screenwriter

In an industry that is based on illusion, the greatest illusion of all is that anyone who can learn to scrawl his name in crayon in kindergarten can write a screenplay.

— ALJEAN HARMETZ, *Esquire,* July 1991

Let me tell you about writing for films. You finish your book. Now, you know where the California state line is? Well, drive to it, take your manuscript and pitch it across. No, on second thought, don't pitch it across. First, let them toss the money over. Then you throw it over, pick up the money and get the hell out of there.

— ERNEST HEMINGWAY, novelist, quoted in *The Book of Hollywood Quotes* by Gary Herman, 1985

Giving your book to Hollywood is like turning your daughter over to a pimp.

— TOM CLANCY, novelist, quoted in the *Los Angeles Times,* February 21, 1995

Hollywood reminds me of a fortress besieged: Everyone outside is trying to get in, and everyone inside is trying to get out.

— RONALD B. TOBIAS, *The Insider's Guide to Writing for Screen and Television,* 1997

The latest collective American wet dream: the salable screenplay.

   — DAVID FREEMAN, "The Great American Screenplay Competition," *Esquire,* June 1980

Generally, these executives reserve all their enthusiasm for movies that have made money; those are the only movies they like.

   — PAULINE KAEL, film critic, *The New Yorker,* June 23, 1980

Contrary to what most people think, the studios aren't really in the entertainment business. They're in the business of earning a profit for their stockholders.

   — NED TANEN, former chief of Universal Studios, quoted in *The Film Year Book* edited by Al Clark, 1985

If I go into Universal and even mention the word art, security forces will come and take me away.

   — TERRY GILLIAM, director and screenwriter of *Brazil*, the award-winning film that was released by Universal only after Gilliam publicly embarrassed the studio by surreptitiously screening the movie for critics himself, quoted in *Time,* December 30, 1985

You have to have a name today to get a script read. The story doesn't count for anything anymore. It's all money, money, money.

   — HOWARD KOCH, one of the original coauthors of *Casablanca,* upon hearing the results of another Charles Ross experiment, *The Wall Street Journal,* November 26, 1982. Ross retyped the script of the classic *Casablanca,* changed the title and the characters' names, and submitted it to 217 agents. It was rejected by 184. (See also *Rejection* for Ross's literary experiments.)

For them not to recognize "Casablanca" is like an English professor not recognizing *Huckleberry Finn* . . . It's pretty discouraging to think that if you sat at home and wrote a screenplay as good as "Casablanca," you might not get anywhere. But on the other hand, one good thing you can say is that the guys who rejected your screenplay were idiots.

   — CHUCK ROSS, freelance writer, quoted in *The Wall Street Journal,* November 26, 1982

Garbage though they turn out, Hollywood writers aren't writing down. That is their best.
— DOROTHY PARKER, quoted in *The Paris Review,* Spring 1956

Don't smell 'em, sell 'em.
— MELINDA JASON, agent, reciting the prevailing shibboleth at many literary agencies, quoted in *Reel Power* by Mark Litwak, 1986

Schmucks with Underwoods.
— JACK WARNER, producer, sentiments about screenwriters, quoted in *Writers in Hollywood 1915–1951* by Ian Hamilton, 1990

(For additional related quotes, see also *Television, Writing for*)

 *Self-Deception*

'Tis a vanity common to all writers, to overvalue their own production.
— JOHN DRYDEN, Dedication to *Examen Poeticum,* 1693

A writer judging his own work is like a deceived husband—he is frequently the last person to appreciate the true state of affairs.
— ROBERT TRAVER, quoted in *Contemporary Novelists* by James Vinson, 1972

It is in the ability to deceive oneself that the greatest talent is shown.
— ANATOLE FRANCE, *La Vie Litteraire,* 1888–1892

As much as we'd all prefer to pretend our calling is a noble one, it's salutary to bear in mind that the last thing this poor old planet needs is another book. The only reason to write anything is because it's something you want to do.
— LAWRENCE BLOCK, *Telling Lies for Fun and Profit,* 1981

If a writer's ego ever wilts, he is ruined. It is the only thing that can sustain him through those lonely months while he is trying to piece together a book out of one recalcitrant word after another. Every morning he has to persuade himself, all over again, that putting words on paper is the most important thing in the world . . . that he has something to say which thousands of people not only will listen to, but pay for . . . Only an egomaniac can believe these things, for they defy all the evidence.

> ━JOHN FISCHER, former book and magazine editor, essay in *Writing in America* edited by John Fischer and Robert B. Silvers, 1960 (Fischer also noted that because of the sheer number of books being published, "the odds therefore are overwhelmingly against any given writer making a ripple on the public consciousness. Or even making a living.")

I advise every young person who aspires to be a writer to cultivate that divine arrogance because without it I doubt you will succeed.

> ━JAMES MICHENER, *James A. Michener's Writer's Handbook*, 1992

You have to believe. It's like religion. The priests who don't have the hardest lives.

> ━DON CARPENTER, novelist, quoted in *Fiction! Interviews with Northern California Novelists* by Dan Tooker, 1976

Of all the abounding illusions one of the grandest may be the illusion possessed by a wide variety of people that "if only I can get my book published" (or having secured a publisher's commitment, "As soon as my book is published,") their lives will pass from one stage of being to another, totally new, higher, sublime.

> ━MARK HARRIS, author, essay in *The New York Times Book Review*, July 11, 1982

The writer must believe that what he is doing is the most important thing in the world. And he must hold to this illusion even when he knows it is not true. If he does not, the work is not worth what it might otherwise have been.

> ━JOHN STEINBECK, novelist, quoted in *The New York Times*, June 2, 1969

⪜ *Self-Publishing* ⪝

Today this tradition . . . of do-it-yourself publishing is too often ignored by writers who imagine that they must be commercially published in order to be proud of their work.

➤ BILL HENDERSON, *The Publish-It-Yourself Handbook*, 1980

Writers get defeated like anyone else. They give up, throw the manuscript in a drawer, never take it out again. I wanted them to realize that they don't have to rely on the publishing establishment to get their books out.

➤ BILL HENDERSON, self-publishing pioneer, quoted in *Wilson Library Bulletin*, November 1979

Historically, the roster of self-publishers has included many names that now appear under publishing's most prestigious imprints.

➤ JUDITH APPELBAUM and NANCY EVANS, *How to Get Happily Published*, 1976

A look at the history of English-language literature reveals that alternative publishing, far from being unusual, is the usual path to prominence of writers whose work does not fit the contemporary commercial mold.

➤ SALLY DENNISON, *Alternative Literary Publishing*, 1984

Today, anybody with a desktop personal computer can be a book publisher.

➤ RICHARD E. BYE, former president, Publishers Marketing Association, *PMA Newsletter*, June 1993

Today, an unknown publisher can produce a book that is every bit as high quality as a book by W. W. Norton . . . That is an enormous change, and you could not say it twenty-five years ago.

➤ TOM ROSS, publishing consultant, quoted in *Publishers Weekly* special anniversary issue, July 1997

That kind of publishing can only get bigger as the number of commercial publishers dwindles.

➤ RICHARD MAREK, editor, responding to reports that the number of new small publishers has skyrocketed, quoted in *The New York Times,* July 9, 1990

Alert New York editors now routinely scan small press catalogues and listen to recommendations from sales reps and booksellers.

➤ PAUL NATHAN, "The Golden Age of Opportunity," *Small Press,* September/October 1997

Self-published works with good track records in the general market often attract the attention on large trade publishers. Peter McWilliams' computer books began that way, as did many other titles.

➤ JANE ADAMS, *How to Sell What You Write,* 1984

The biggies—those publishers that previously rejected your work—just may decide to reverse their decision. Self-publishing can be the springboard to lucrative contracts with traditional publishers who were afraid to gamble before. Once the marketability of your work has been proven, they will be eager to take it off your hands.

➤ TOM ROSS and MARILYN ROSS, *The Complete Guide to Self-Publishing,* 1985

Small publishers and self-publishers have real advantages over the dinosaurs. We're fast. (We can get a book on the market in weeks, not months.) We're dedicated. (No three-hour spritzer lunches for us.) We're not afraid of hard work. (Well, at least we're willing to overcome the fear.) We have something to lose. (Our life savings, usually.) And we believe passionately in what we sell. (More often than not, we wrote it.)

➤ PETER MCWILLIAMS, "The Revolution in Self-Publishing," *Writer's Digest,* October 1984

The big New York trade publishers may have more promotional connections than you but with a whole stable of books to push, your book may get lost in the shuffle. At least if you self-publish, you can be sure your book is in the hands of someone who cares—you.

— DAN POYNTER and MINDY BINGHAM, *Is There a Book Inside You?*, 1991

The self-publisher really has control of his or her destiny to a much larger degree than does a writer merely submitting a manuscript [to a publisher].

— DAN POYNTER, author, *The Self-Publishing Manual,* quoted in *The Mother Earth News,* July/August 1985

For a great many self-publishers, the primary reason for self-publication is control. If you sell your book to a publisher, matters are taken pretty much out of your hands. Someone else takes over the editing . . . Someone else designs the book . . . Someone else decides the print run size. Somebody else makes the decision regarding the promotion of the book. Somebody else decides how long the book will be promoted, and as a usual thing, large publishers move on to other books after a year.

— PATRICIA J. BELL, *The Prepublishing Handbook,* 1992

Self-publishing means setting up a small business. Investment capital must be found to start with, then the writer must take time away from his or her writing to do the work of publishing and distributing the book, often being forced to learn the skills needed for successful publishing as he goes along.

— SALLY DENNISON, *Alternative Literary Publishing,* 1984

Ultimately, self-publishing is a high-stakes game. Books often fail, but successful writers can actually make more money from a self-published book than they could through a big publishing company.

— JOHN TESSITORE, "Desktop Publishing Wave Brings Tide of New Authors to Bookstore Shelves," *Christian Science Monitor,* July 11, 1996

Why accept 6% to 10% in royalties when you can have 35%?
  ⟞ DAN POYNTER, *The Self-Publishing Manual,* 1999

Are you the type of person who wants to be behind the wheel rather than go along for the ride?
  ⟞ TOM ROSS and MARILYN ROSS, *The Complete Guide to Self-Publishing,* 1985

A writer who publishes himself is a horse's ass.
  ⟞ **HOWARD FAST, novelist, who went bankrupt after self-publishing several books when he felt ostracized by publishers during the McCarthy era, quoted in** *Writing for Your Life* **edited by Sybil Steinberg, 1992**

If you are prepared to function as your own producer and marketer as well as a writer, have a sound business plan for your Product, and can raise the money or fund it from other writing projects that Buyers pay you for, do not dismiss it out of hand.
  ⟞ JANE ADAMS, *How to Sell What You Write,* 1984

Publishing is not difficult. In fact, it may be easier than dealing with a publisher. The job of the publishing manager is not to perform every task, but to see that everything gets done.
  ⟞ DAN POYNTER, *The Self-Publishing Manual,* 1999

The only hard part comes when you try to market the finished product. If it's any consolation, even the big publishing companies have trouble with this end of the business.
  ⟞ STEPHEN GOLDIN and KATHLEEN SKY, *The Business of Being a Writer,* 1982

A self-publisher will very often be able to reach local, regional, or narrow markets far less expensively and more profitably than will a commercial publisher . . . A book that may be quite properly seen as a foolish gamble by a commercial publisher may be a perfectly sensible candidate for publication by its own author.
  ⟞ DAVID M. BROWNSTONE and IRENE M. FRANCK, *The Self-Publishing Handbook,* 1985

Self-publishing works best with how-to books and carefully targeted niche markets.

▬ ANNE KATES SMITH, *U.S. News & World Report,* June 8, 1992

One of the biggest mistakes [self-publishers make] is a poor choice of subject. The average person does not really think about the marketability of their subject before they get started.

▬ MARILYN ROSS, *Griffith's Spotlight* newsletter, November 1987

Before you make any editorial decisions, you should always ask yourself the question: "Who will buy the book, and why?"

▬ JOHN KREMER, *1,001 Ways to Market Your Book,* 1999

Self-publishing is not for everyone, nor is it equally suitable for all types of books.

▬ DAVID M. BROWNSTONE and IRENE M. FRANCK, *The Self-Publishing Handbook,* 1985

Self-publishing will consume all the time, concentration and energy you've got. If you don't want to commit your soul to the project, forget it.

▬ MARK ALVAREZ, *Home-Office Computing,* February 1992

If your book doesn't look as good as a book published by Doubleday, don't bother.

▬ RICHARD PAUL EVANS, author of *The Christmas Box* (1995), quoted in *Writer's Digest,* December 1998

Self-publishing should not be confused with vanity press publication.

▬ BILL HENDERSON, president, Pushcart Press, "Independent Publishing: Today and Yesterday," essay in *Perspectives on Publishing* edited by Philip G. Altbach and Sheila McVey, 1976

Libraries as well as bookstores and critics avoid vanity books like the plague. So should you.

▬ JANE ADAMS, *How to Sell What You Write,* 1984

The vanity publisher is out to milk you for all he can get . . . He demands legal control of the books you paid him to print, makes only the most rudimentary attempts to sell copies, and then makes you pay him again to get the books back.

➤ STEPHEN GOLDIN and KATHLEEN SKY, *The Business of Being a Writer,* 1982

In two years, my [vanity] publisher only sold four books out of 2,000. Any kid on the street could peddle my books around the neighborhood and sell a dozen in one evening.

Authors beware! Go directly to a reputable printing company that specializes in books. Accept three, four, even five separate bids on your complete manuscript. Don't be taken by a vanity press.

➤ HOWARD HENRY MOST, "A Warning to Writers," *Los Angeles Times,* February 8, 1981

If [bookstore owners and editors] learn that you've published a book with a vanity house, they'll not only not going to be impressed, they'll probably consider you a naïve, self-indulgent rube.

➤ SCOTT EDELSTEIN, *100 Things Every Writer Needs to Know,* 1999

"Self-published books don't sell" doesn't mean [bookstores] are not going to take your book. It simply means, "C'mon. Prove us wrong."

➤ Unidentified self-publisher, quoted in *Wilson Library Bulletin,* April 1978

 *Spelling*

I have no respect for a person who can't spell a word more than one way.

➤ MARK TWAIN, novelist, quoted in *Comedy Writing for Television and Hollywood* by Milt Josefsberg, 1987

Success and Failure

Success is never final and failure never fatal. It's courage that counts.

➤ GEORGE R. TILTON, educator, quoted in *The World's Best Thoughts About Success & Failure* compiled by Eugene Raudsepp, 1981

To me, a real "failure" is to write a bad book. A public failure is to have a book that is not a success—that's not the same thing.

➤ FRAN LEBOWITZ, humorist, quoted in *Harper's Bazaar,* July 1983

The worst that can happen to the writer who tries and fails—unless he has inflated or mystical notions of what it is to be a novelist—is that he will discover, for him, writing is not the best place to seek joy and satisfaction. More people fail at becoming successful businessmen than fail at becoming artists.

➤ JOHN GARDNER, *On Becoming a Novelist,* 1983

More great Americans were failures than they were successes. They mostly spent their lives not having a buyer for what they had for sale.

➤ GERTRUDE STEIN, *Everybody's Autobiography,* 1937

F. Scott Fitzgerald died thinking he was an absolute failure. Today he's one of the icons of American fiction.

➤ IRWIN SHAW, novelist, quoted in *Counterpoint* compiled and edited by Roy Newquist, 1964

No one knows what he can do till he tries.

➤ PUBLILIUS SYRUS, *Maxim 786,* first century B.C.

My view is that to sit back and let fate play its hand out and never influence it at all is not the way man was meant to operate.

➤ JOHN GLENN, U.S. senator and astronaut, quoted in *New York* magazine, January 31, 1983

On the door to success it says Push and Pull.

➤ Yiddish proverb

Success is the child of Audacity.

➤ BENJAMIN DISRAELI, *The Wondrous Tale of Aloy. The Rise of Iskander,* 1833

Only those who dare to fail greatly can ever achieve greatly.

➤ ROBERT F. KENNEDY, *To Seek a Newer World,* 1967

To follow, without halt, one's aim: That's the secret of success.

➤ ANNA PAVLOVA, *Pavlova: A Biography* edited by A. H. Franks, 1956

Success . . . depends upon knowing how long it will take to succeed.

➤ CHARLES-LOUIS MONTESQUIEU, French political philosopher, *Pensees Diverses,* 1866

The people who succeed in the writing business are the ones who don't take rejection very seriously, but who keep on patiently building their skills and their careers. Become one of these writers if you can.

➤ SCOTT EDELSTEIN, *100 Things Every Writer Needs to Know,* 1999

The secret of success in life is known only to those who have not succeeded.

➤ JOHN CHURTON COLLINS, English scholar and critic, quoted in *A Treasury of English Aphorisms* edited by Logan Pearsall Smith, 1928

Successful men usually snatch success from seeming failure. If they know there is such a word as defeat they will not admit it. They may be whipped, but they are not aware of it. That is why they succeed.

➤ A. P. GOUTHEY, quoted in *The World's Best Thoughts on Success & Failure* compiled by Eugene Raudsepp, 1981

Successful men and women . . . don't consider the odds. They just sneak up at night and cut their own holes in the fence.
— WELLS ROOT, *Writing the Script,* 1980

The greatest pleasure in life is doing what people say you cannot do.
— WALTER BAGEHOT, *Literary Studies,* 1905–1907

You'll make mistakes. Some . . . will call them failures, but I have learned that failure is really God's way of saying, "Excuse me, you're moving in the wrong direction."
— OPRAH WINFREY, talk show host, 1997 commencement address at Wellesley College, quoted in *Time,* June 16, 1997

You only fail if you stop writing.
— RAY BRADBURY, novelist, quoted in *The Writer's Digest Guide to Good Writing,* 1994

As a writing coach, I can testify that most writers fail . . . [because] they can't stay focused.
— JAMES N. FREY, "The Mother of All Attitudes," in *The Portable Writers' Conference* edited by Stephen Blake Mettee, 1997

For every person who will say yes, there are twenty who will say no. For a positive response you must find the twenty-first person.
— CHUCK REAVES, *The Theory of 21: Finding the Power to Succeed,* 1983

Success makes us intolerant of failure, and failure makes us intolerant of success.
— WILLIAM FEATHER, *The Business of Life,* 1949

[*Definition*] Success, n. The one unpardonable sin against one's fellows.
— AMBROSE BIERCE, *The Devil's Dictionary,* 1941

The only reward to be expected from the cultivation of literature is contempt if one fails and hatred if one succeeds.
— VOLTAIRE, French philosopher, in letter to Mlle. Quinault, 1763

The people simply cannot endure success over too long a period of time. It has to be destroyed. If a person survives, then he goes on and comes back stronger than ever. I know, because I've been through this three times.

➤ TRUMAN CAPOTE, novelist, quoted in *Conversations With American Writers* by Charles Ruas, 1985

There is always something about your success that displeases even your best friends.

➤ OSCAR WILDE, English humorist, quoted in *The World's Best Thoughts on Success & Failure* compiled by Eugene Raudsepp, 1981

Success may come at any stage of a novelist's life.

➤ JOHN BRAINE, *Writing a Novel*, 1974

I never wrote anything that was published until I was forty.

➤ JAMES MICHENER, novelist, quoted in *The Complete Guide to Writing Fiction* by Barnaby Conrad, 1990

Most successful members of society have broken the traditional age-rules. They have done things when they wanted to do them and have ignored any imagined limitations on them.

➤ DESMOND MORRIS, *The Book of Ages*, 1984

As every publisher knows, good books—books of high literary or scholarly merit—fail as often, if not more often, than do books of questionable merit.

➤ CURTIS G. BENJAMIN, *A Candid Critique of Book Publishing*, 1977

Many books fail which would have succeeded two or three years earlier, or two or three years later, because the mood of the public—the directions in which the winds of interest blow—changes so rapidly.

➤ MAXWELL E. PERKINS, editor, letter to novelist Arthur Train, June 21, 1938, cited in *Editor to Author: The Letters of Maxwell E. Perkins* selected and edited by John Hall Wheelock, 1950

Success is what sells.

━ ANDY WARHOL, artist, quoted in *Conversations With American Writers* by Charles Ruas, 1985

In the arts there are no A's awarded for effort.

━ JOHN BRAINE, *Writing a Novel,* 1974

A writer cannot choose when or if success will come. You can only do your best and be prepared for your moment of opportunity by writing, writing—and then writing some more.

━ NOREEN AYRES, novelist, quoted in *Unstoppable* by Cynthia Kersey, 1998

There is only one success—to be able to spend your life in your own way.

━ CHRISTOPHER MORLEY, *Where the Blues Begin,* 1922

 *Talent*

Literature is an occupation in which you have to keep proving your talent to people who have none.

━ JULES RENARD, *Journal,* 1887

It strikes me now and then that talent may be one of the least important variables in the writing business. People without superabundance of talent succeed anyhow. People with tons of talent never get anywhere. It happens all the time. And it happens, I guess, in every field or endeavor.

━ LAWRENCE BLOCK, *Telling Lies for Fun and Profit,* 1981

The luck of having talent is not enough; one must also have a talent for luck.

━ Attributed to HECTOR BERLIOZ, composer

Luck is the residue of design.

— Attributed to BRANCH RICKEY, former owner, St. Louis Cardinals

It took me fifteen years to discover I had no talent for writing, but I couldn't give it up because by that time I was too famous.

— ROBERT BENCHLEY, *Benchley Beside Himself,* 1943

Everyone has a talent. What is rare is the courage to follow that talent to the dark places where it leads.

— ERICA JONG, "The Artist As Housewife," *The First Ms. Reader* edited by Francine Klagsburn, 1973

It is my belief that talent is plentiful, and that what is lacking is staying power.

— DORIS LESSING, "Into the Labyrinth," essay in *Author! Author!* edited by Richard Findlater, 1984

A great deal of talent is lost to the world for the want of a little courage.

— SYDNEY SMITH, *Elementary Sketches of Moral Philosophy,* 1850

A talent somewhat above mediocrity, shrewd and not too sensitive, is more likely to rise in the world than genius, which is apt to be perturbable and wear itself out before fruition.

— Attributed to CHARLES HOOTON COOLEY, social scientist

Nearly everything in the scheme of things works to dull a first-rate talent.

— NORMAN MAILER, novelist, quoted in *Writers at Work,* Third Series, 1967

Great practitioners in any field make it look easy, so bystanders murmur in awe about talent. What the bystander never sees is the agony of effort, study, and practice that made the final performance appear effortless—the fruits of a professional attitude.

— JACK M. BICKHAM, *Writing Novels That Sell,* 1996

If I'm a lousy writer, then a helluva lot of people have lousy taste.
> ⬿ GRACE METALIUS, author, *Peyton Place,* quoted in *The Great Quotations* by George Seldes, 1967

⬿ *Television, Writing for* ⬿

Literature has taken a back seat to television, don't you think?
> ⬿ TENNESSEE WILLIAMS, playwright, quoted in *The Paris Review,* Fall 1981

Television, the scorned stepchild of drama, may well be the basic theater of our century.
> ⬿ Attributed to PADDY CHAFEVSKY, novelist, screenwriter, and television writer

To truly understand television, you must first unlearn a popular misconception. Except in the strictest technological sense, television is not primarily a communications medium. It is primarily a sales medium. In an interesting reversal of the normal box office concept, it sells its audience to the actual and only customers, the advertisers.
> ⬿ STEWART BRONFELD, *Writing for Film and Television,* 1981

The reason that I think that most TV comedy is so awful is because people write it with an audience in mind. Because somebody tells them who is watching it and who has to like it. That is a backwards way to write.
> ⬿ FRAN LEBOWITZ, humorist, interview with William A. Gordon, 1983

TV sponsors are trying to win customers, not alienate them; so most TV humor is "safe."
> ⬿ STEVE ALLEN with JAN WOLLMAN, *How to Be Funny,* 1987

Television demands a lot of material in a short time. Sometimes that doesn't afford the luxury of polishing each little gem to the luster that you would prefer. The producers knock on your office door and ask, "Is it done?", not "Is it funny?"

➤ GENE PERRET, *How to Write and Sell Your Sense of Humor,* 1982

In TV . . . you learn to say, "It's just another play, it's just another movie." We mustn't don the mantle of posterity every time we sit down to a typewriter. You learn to say, "Let the rest of the world worry about posterity. I'll just go on with what I want to do." You learn a lot of things.

➤ PADDY CHAFEVSKY, quoted in *The Craft of the Screenwriter* by John Brady, 1981

All the really great [TV] series have been the vision of one or two people working together creating the show.

➤ LINDA BLOODWORTH-THOMASON, *Designing Women* creator and executive producer, criticizing what is known in the industry as "gang writing," or sitcoms written by committee, quoted in the *Los Angeles Times,* December 6, 1998

Fame is an unlikely result of writing for television. How many television writers can you name?

➤ STUART M. KAMINSKY, *Writing for Television,* 1988

Television is so low-grade not because talent is in short supply (the insider's excuse) or because the producers want to make dreck (the critic's exasperated judgment) but because it doesn't have to be any better.

➤ PAT AUFDERHEIDE, cultural critic, reviewing Tod Gitlin's *Inside Prime Time* (1983) in *In These Times*

Nobody's setting out to make shit, but there are just so many Jim Brookses and Allen Burnses. Television would be wonderful if it were only on Wednesday night.

➤ GRANT TINKER, NBC executive, quoted in *Inside Prime Time* by Tod Gitlin, 1983

Commercial television makes so much money doing its worst that it cannot afford to do its best.

— Attributed to FRED FRIENDLY, former president, CBS

Disparaging television has long been a favorite national pastime—second in popularity only to watching it.

— "Television Looks at Itself," *Harper's,* March 1985

The biggest best seller in modern times was probably *Gone With the Wind.* People who never read a book in their lives had to read that—and what was the sale? Maybe 20 million copies, the absolute saturation point. Put that against the total population! Compare it with the television audience!

— Attributed to ROBERT GIROUX, publisher, Farrar, Straus & Giroux

I just think it's very nice for our industry and for our country as a whole that in 1998 an award in comedy writing can be won by a Gentile, and I thank you.

— PETER TOLAN, accepting a best writing award (shared with Garry Shandling) for the *Larry Sanders Show,* Emmy Awards broadcast on NBC, September 12, 1998

 Wit

True wit is rare, and a thousand barbed arrows fall at the feet of the archer for every one that flies.

— WILLIAM ZINSSER, *On Writing Well,* 1976

There's a hell of a distance between wisecracking and wit. Wit has truth to it; wisecracking is simply calisthenics with words.

— DOROTHY PARKER, humorist, quoted in *The Paris Review,* Spring 1956

Wit is the salt of conversation, not the food.
➤ WILLIAM HAZLITT, *Lectures on the English Comic Writer,* 1951

There's no possibility of being witty without a little ill-nature.
➤ Attributed to RICHARD SHERIDAN, playwright

Impropriety is the soul of wit.
➤ W. SOMERSET MAUGHAM, *The Moon and Sixpence,* 1935

Wit is educated insolence.
➤ ARISTOTLE, *The Basic Works of Aristotle* edited by Richard McKeon, 1941

[*Definition of a witticism*] A sharp and clever remark, usually quoted and seldom noted; what the Philistine is pleased to call a "joke."
➤ AMBROSE BIERCE, *The Devil's Dictionary,* 1911

Wit is the rarest quality to be met with among people of education.
➤ WILLIAM HAZLITT, *Characteristics,* 1821–1822

You know, someone once said that Dorothy Parker had wasted her life wisecracking. I really can't think of a better use of a life.
➤ FRAN LEBOWITZ, humorist, quoted in *New Times,* July 10, 1978

Word Economy

I prefer to underwrite. Simple, clear as a country creek.
➤ Attributed to TRUMAN CAPOTE, novelist

The writer does the most, who gives his reader the most knowledge, and takes from him the least time.
➤ CHARLES CALEB COLTON, Preface to *Iacon,* 1825

It is my ambition to say in ten sentences what everyone else says in a whole book—what everyone else does not say in a whole book.
➤ FRIEDRICH NIETZSCHE, *Twilight of the Idols,* 1888

Most of the time less is more.
➤ DONALD MURRAY, *Writing for Your Readers,* 1983

The Ten Commandments contained 297 words . . . The Bill of Rights is stated in 438 words . . . Lincoln's Gettysburg Address contained 266 words.
A recent federal directive to regulate the price of cabbage contains 26,911 words.
➤ Unknown

Even the second coming of Christ doesn't merit more than 600 words.
➤ Attributed to FRANK GARAFOLO, business writer

A sentence should contain no unnecessary words for the same reason that a machine should have no unnecessary parts.
➤ WILLIAM STRUNK, JR., *The Elements of Style,* 1959

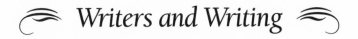 *Writers and Writing*

Writing is a dog's life, but the only life worth living.
➤ GUSTAVE FLAUBERT, French novelist, quoted in *The Crown Treasury of Relevant Quotations* by Edward F. Murphy, 1978

I love being a writer. What I can't stand is the paperwork.
➤ PETER DE VRIES, novelist, quoted in *The Literary Life and Other Curiosities* by Robert Hendrickson, 1981

The test of a vocation is the love of the drudgery it involves.

➤ LOGAN PEARSALL SMITH, *Afterthoughts*, 1931

What no wife of a writer can understand is that a writer is working when he is staring out the window.

➤ Attributed to BURTON RASCOE, former literary editor, *New York Herald Tribune*

The true artist will let his wife starve, his children go barefoot, his mother drudge for her living at seventy, sooner than work at anything but his art.

➤ GEORGE BERNARD SHAW, *Man and Superman*, 1907

Never let a domestic quarrel ruin a day's writing. If you can't start the next day fresh, get rid of your wife.

➤ MARIO PUZO, novelist/screenwriter, quoted in *The 637 Best Things Anybody Ever Said* edited by Robert Byrne, 1982

Most people who earn their livings as writers are a little nuts—perhaps not certifiable—but certainly not exactly your average American.

➤ BILL ADLER, *Inside Publishing*, 1982

All writers are more or less crazy—and the only argument I'll listen to is whether they were crazy to start with or got that way from writing.

➤ ALLEN MARPLE, short-story writer, columnist, and former editor, *Collier's*, quoted in *Writer's Digest*, December 1987

Few men have ever [depended upon their pen for daily bread]. Few men have ever done it happily . . . Most writers, from Shakespeare down, have had other resources.

➤ HENRY HOLT, publisher, *The Atlantic*, November 1905

Sir, no man but a blockhead ever wrote except for money.

➤ SAMUEL JOHNSON, English writer, lexicographer, and critic, quoted in *Life of Johnson* by James Boswell, 1791

Dr. Johnson . . . wrote one of the minor masterpieces of English literature to get enough money to pay for his mother's funeral. Balzac and Dickens without shame wrote for money.

— W. SOMERSET MAUGHAM, *Great Novelists and Their Novels,* 1948

If you want to get rich from writing, write the sort of thing that's read by persons who move their lips when they're reading to themselves.

— Attributed to DONALD MARQUIS, newspaper columnist

Writers rarely become rich and famous because of the quality of their work. They become rich and famous because of the nature of their work.

— GARRY PROVOST, *Writer's Digest,* March 1986

If writers were good businessmen, they'd have too much sense to be writers.

— IRWIN S. COBB, playwright, quoted in *Peter's Quotations* by Dr. Laurence J. Peter, 1976

Writing is bosh. There is only one way to make money at writing, and that is to marry a publisher's daughter.

— Advice given to novelist George Orwell by a Russian friend, quoted in *Down and Out in Paris and London* by George Orwell, 1949

The life of a writer is usually one of permanent insecurity.

— JAMES T. FARRELL, *James T. Farrell: Literary Essays, 1954–1977* collected and edited by Jack Alan Robins, 1976

The profession of letters is, after all, the only one in which one can make no money without being ridiculous.

— JULES RENARD, *Journal,* 1887

It is better to have a permanent income than to be fascinating.

— Attributed to OSCAR WILDE, English novelist, playwright, and critic

Crime does not pay—enough.

> ➤ CLAYTON RAWSON, founder, Mystery Writers of America, quoted in *American Heritage Dictionary of American Quotations* compiled by Hugh Rawson and Margaret Miner, 1997

Write without pay until somebody offers you pay. If nobody offers within three years the candidate may look upon the circumstance with the most implicit confidence as the sign that sawing wood is what he was intended for.

> ➤ MARK TWAIN, novelist, quoted in *The Wit and Wisdom of Mark Twain* edited by Alex Ayres, 1987

As a younger man I wrote for eight years without ever earning a nickel, which is a long apprenticeship, but in that time I learned a lot about my trade.

> ➤ JAMES MICHENER, novelist, quoted in *Conversations With Writers II* edited by Matthew J. Bruccoli, 1977

I never write—indeed, am physically incapable of writing—anything I don't think will be paid for.

> ➤ TRUMAN CAPOTE, novelist, quoted in *The Paris Review,* Spring/Summer 1957

This isn't the Lawn Tennis Association, where you just play for the thrill of it.

> ➤ JIMMY BRESLIN, columnist, quoted in *The Self-Publishing Manual* by Dan Poynter, 1999

Why shouldn't writers live well? They contribute the most precious commodities to the world: the ideas and values that shape society. Isn't a professional entitled to be paid for his work?

> ➤ PAT KUBIS and BOB HOWLAND, *Writing Fiction, Nonfiction and How to Publish,* 1985

No one ever told a story well standing up or fasting.

> ➤ HONORE DE BALZAC, novelist, quoted in *Barnes & Noble Book of Quotations* edited by Robert I. Fitzhenry, 1983

Always we come upon this feeling, ridiculous, senseless and baseless—that it is beneath the dignity of an author to manage his business matters as a man of business should.

> ━ WALTER BESANT, "Commercial Values," essay in *Author! Author!* edited by Richard Findlater, 1984

No one . . . ever thought of reproaching the barrister, the solicitor, the physician, the surgeon, the painter, the sculptor, the actor, the singer, the musician, the composer, the architect, the chemist, the physicist, the engineer, the professor, the teacher, the clergyman, or any other kind of brain worker that one can mention, with taking fees or salaries or money for his work.

> ━ WALTER BESANT, "Commercial Values," essay in *Author! Author!* edited by Richard Findlater, 1984

There exists a stupid literary tradition . . . that a hungry writer is the best writer—an empty stomach and slum dwelling being considered most conducive to good books, honest books, uncorrupted books. Revolting nonsense, I say . . . The really hungry writer, I truly believe, is the one most susceptible to corruption and dishonesty, for he has a problem that must intrude on his creativity. The problem is: he must eat. And to eat, he must often put aside writing as he pleases, to write potboilers for the marketplace, to write what he is told to write.

The writer who has money, enough or a lot, has to compromise with no one, do nothing he does not want to. He can afford to write as he pleases.

> ━ IRVING WALLACE, novelist, quoted in *Conversations* by Roy Newquist, 1967

Even "successful" writers, when their incomes are averaged out over a working lifetime, do well to make a postman's salary, without the benefits.

> ━ JAYNE ANN PHILLIPS, novelist and short-story writer, "Why She Writes," essay in *Why I Write: Thoughts on the Craft of Fiction* edited by Will Blythe, 1998

I believe the saddest news one has to give any young writer just setting out is that very few good writers are able to support themselves by their writing.

➤ PETER TAYLOR, *The Writer's Craft,* 1982

To say that writers, as a group, are underpaid is a grotesque understatement. The fact is that most of us cannot survive on what we earn from writing, despite the attention that the select few receive from million-dollar contracts.

➤ *National Writers Union Guide to Freelance Rates and Standard Practice*

I don't want to take up literature in a money-making spirit, or be very anxious about making large profits, but selling it at a loss is another thing altogether, and an amusement I cannot well afford.

➤ **LEWIS CARROLL, English author and mathematician, in a letter to his publisher, quoted in *Letters to Macmillan* edited by Simon Nowell-Smith, 1967**

The profession of book writing makes horse racing seem like a solid, stable business.

➤ **JOHN STEINBECK, novelist, quoted in *Newsweek,* December 24, 1962**

Authorship is a fantasy, a dream of most aspirants. It's a glittering notion, a mirage with their name on the title page.

➤ WILLIAM TARG, *Indecent Pleasures,* 1975

The urge to be published may be top among human vanities.

➤ ARTHUR PLOTNIK, *Honk If You're a Writer,* 1992

Writing is the toughest thing I've ever done.

➤ **Attributed to RICHARD M. NIXON, former President of the United States**

I haven't met many writers who feel comfortable with writing.

➤ **Attributed to KAY BOYLE, novelist and short-story writer**

Every writer I know has trouble writing.

— JOSEPH HELLER, novelist, quoted in *The Truth About Fiction Writing* by William Appel and Denise Sterrs, 1997

Since writing is the worst part of being a writer this can be a very depressing experience.

— JAMES ATLAS, *Vanity Fair,* September 1985

The most glamorous, brilliant, prestigious authors still sit by themselves with their tortured psyches and numbed fingers.

— IRVING WALLACE, novelist, quoted in *Conversations* by Roy Newquist, 1967

Writing is so difficult that I often feel that writers, having had their hell on earth, will escape all punishment hereafter.

— JESSAMYN WEST, *To See the Dream,* 1957

Writing is the opposite of sex. It's only good when it's over.

— SIDNEY ZION, novelist, quoted in *Publishers Weekly,* May 5, 1990

Writing is the loneliest job in the world.

— FANNIE HURST, novelist, quoted in *Simpson's Contemporary Quotations,* 1988

It's as lonesome at the end or on the mountaintops as it is at the beginning or in the valleys.

— Attributed to MICHAEL DRURY, novelist

I don't think loneliness is the word. John Graves said writing is "anti-life." I'm forty-five years old. I've been writing full-time since I was sixteen. I've been writing almost every day for thirty years, and as I look back with a degree of resentment, I realize that I literally lifted chunks of my life out for drafts of things, some of which got published and some didn't.

— TOM GUANE, novelist, regretting what he called "a hole in my life," quoted in *Conversations With American Novelists* edited by Kay Bonetti, Greg Michalson, Speer Morgan, Jo Sapp, and Sam Stowers, 1997

I've always thought people write because they are not living properly.

➤ BERYL BAINBRIDGE, novelist/actress, quoted in London's *Daily Telegraph*, September 10, 1996

No one in his right mind would sit down to write a book if he were a well-adjusted, happy man.

➤ JAY MCINERNEY, novelist, quoted in London's *Independent Sunday*, April 19, 1992

I'm only really alive when I'm writing.

➤ Attributed to TENNESSEE WILLIAMS, playwright

Writing is like making love. You have to practice to be good at it.

➤ MORRIS WEST, "How to Write a Novel," *The Writer*, May 1977

Writing, like making love, is more fun when you know what you're doing.

➤ EILEEN JENSEN, "You Can Get There From Here," *The Writer*, June 1973

They're there, they're mine, they're my children.

➤ NORMAN MAILER, novelist, referring to his books, quoted in *Writer's Digest*, October 1983

Writing books is the closest men ever come to childbearing.

➤ NORMAN MAILER, *Conversations With Norman Mailer*, 1988

If we had to say what writing is, we would have to define it essentially as an act of courage.

➤ Attributed to CYNTHIA OZICK, novelist

[*Definition*] The art of applying the seat of the pants to the seat of the chair.

➤ Attributed to MARY HEATON VORSE, journalist

Oh! It's a real horse's ass business.

➤ Attributed to JOHN STEINBECK, novelist

The most important part of the writer's anatomy is not the brain, where ideas are born, or the hands that transfer those ideas into concrete form, but the backside . . . In my experience, the big difference between published and unpublished writers is that published writers sit down and write.

→ PHILLIP M. MARGOLIN, "How to Deal With Non-Writer's Block," *1995 Writer's Handbook*

[*Definition*] One of the cruelest of professions.

→ JAMES T. FARRELL, *James T. Farrell: Literary Essays 1954–1977* collected and edited by Jack Alan Robins, 1976

Writing . . . is but a different name for conversation.

→ LAWRENCE STERNE, *Tristram Shandy,* 1760–1767

It's a crazy business, anyway, locking yourself in a room and inventing conversations, no way for a grownup to behave.

→ JOHN LEONARD, *Esquire,* November 1975

It's queer for a live human being, endowed with intelligence, to spend waking hours of a very mortal life cooped up in a room, not talking to anybody, just scribbling words on a page.

→ JOHN BARTH, novelist, quoted in *First Person Singular* compiled by Joyce Carol Oates, 1983

In order to be a good writer, you've got to be a bad boss. Self-discipline and stamina are the two major arms in a writer's arsenal.

→ Attributed to LEON URIS, novelist

What a writer needs most is energy. It's the most important thing you can have if you're really going to be a writer and outlast the bastards who'll try and stop you.

→ FREDERICK BUSCH, quoting his father, attorney Benjamin Busch, *A Dangerous Profession: A Book About the Writing Life,* 1998

Everybody can write; writers can't do anything else.

→ MIGNON MCLAUGHLIN, *The Neurotic's Notebook,* 1963

I think the writer in America doesn't enjoy a very exalted position; he's really a third-rate citizen.

➤ JAMES MICHENER, novelist, quoted in *Conversations With Writers II* edited by Matthew J. Bruccoli, 1976

The novelist in America . . . is positively regarded as a kind of freak unless he retreats to the university or hits the jackpot in the mass media.

➤ Attributed to HOWARD SWADOS, novelist and short-story writer

Writers are a little below clowns and a little above trained seals. God help the world if writers ever took control.

➤ JOHN STEINBECK, novelist, quoted in a 1961 Associated Press interview, reprinted in *Conversations With John Steinbeck* edited by Thomas Fensch, 1988

A writer has no choice but to be a writer.

➤ BILL BUFORD, *The New Yorker,* June 26 & July 3, 1995

The only reason for being a professional writer is that you can't help it.

➤ LEO ROSTEN, novelist/screenwriter, quoted in *Contemporary Novelists* by James Vinson, 1976

I think all writing is a disease. You can't stop it.

➤ WILLIAM CARLOS WILLIAMS, poet and novelist, quoted in *Newsweek,* January 7, 1957

It's a hell of a disease to be born with.

➤ Attributed to ERNEST HEMINGWAY, novelist

Against the disease of writing one must take special precautions.

➤ PIERRE ABELARD, *Letter to Heloise,* 1036

I am a writer. I use people for what I write. Let the world beware.

➤ Sharon Stone, in the 1991 movie *Basic Instinct,* screenplay by JOE ESZTERHAS

Every great and original writer, in proportion as he is great and original, must create the taste by which he is relished.

> ━ WILLIAM WORDSWORTH, English poet, letter to Lady Beaumont, May 21, 1807, quoted in the Preface to *Lyrical Ballads*, Second Edition, 1907

A writer is in the end not his books, but his myth—and that myth is in the keeping of others.

> ━ V. S. NAIPAUL, "Steinbeck in Monterey," essay in *The Overcrowded Barracoon*, 1972

This business about having spent 50 years writing it is pure nonsense.

> ━ HELEN HOOVER SANTMYER, novelist, dismissing one of the helpful myths that helped make her . . . *And Ladies of the Club* (1982) a major discovery and a publishing sensation, quoted in Cleveland's *Plain Dealer,* January 29, 1984

People stick a label on you and thirty years later, it's still there because they haven't the patience to look and see that it no longer fits.

> ━ Attributed to JOHN O'HARA, short-story writer

An author is always unconsciously fighting for an image and, when he gets one, consciously fighting against it.

> ━ Attributed to J. P. DONLEAVY, novelist, playwright, and short-story writer

The writer's own responsibility is to his art. He will be completely ruthless if he is a good one. He has a dream. It anguishes him so much he must get rid of it. He has no peace until then.

> ━ WILLIAM FAULKNER, novelist, quoted in *The Paris Review,* Spring 1966

Writers are always selling somebody out.

> ━ JOAN DIDION, Preface to *Slouching Towards Bethlehem,* 1968

You write a hit the same way you write a flop.

> ━ Attributed to WILLIAM SAROYAN, novelist

I'm basically a treacherous person with no sense of loyalty. I'd write openly about my sainted mother's sex life for art.

— SUSAN BRAUDY, author, *What the Movies Made Me Do* (1985), quoted in *Interview,* September 1985

A writer is a writer, period. He can be a fascist but still be an important writer.

— NAT HENTOFF, *Publishers Weekly,* April 11, 1986

He [the writer] is not exempt from the normal obligation to be a decent human being.

— HERBERT GOLD, novelist, quoted in *Esquire,* August 1986

Writers are cannibals . . . It is a terrible thing to be the friend, the acquaintance, [or] the relative of a writer.

— CYNTHIA OZICK, speaking at an Authors Guild symposium, October 19, 1998, quoted in the *Author's Guild Bulletin,* Winter 1999

There is no rule on how to write. Sometimes it comes easily and perfectly. Sometimes it's like drilling rock and blasting it out with charges.

— ERNEST HEMINGWAY, novelist, in a letter to editor Charles Poore, 1953, in *Ernest Hemingway: Selected Letters, 1917–1961* edited by Carlos Baker, 1981

Writing a book is an adventure. To begin with, it is a toy and an amusement. Then it becomes a mistress, then it becomes a master, then it becomes a tyrant. The last phase is that just as you are about to be reconciled to your servitude, you kill the monster and fling it to the public.

— WINSTON CHURCHILL, British prime minister, quoted in *The New York Times Magazine,* November 13, 1949

Great writers leave us not just their work, but a way of looking at things.

— ELIZABETH JANEWAY, novelist and critic, quoted in *The New York Times,* January 31, 1965

The books come and go. But the kids. That's what I'm leaving.

— ERMA BOMBECK, humorist, quoted in *People,* February 13, 1984

A good writer is one who produces books that people read . . . So if I'm selling millions, I'm good.

— JACQUELINE SUSANN, novelist, quoted in *Lovely Me: The Life of Jacqueline Susann* by Barbara Seaman, 1987

Good writers have two things in common: they prefer being understood to being admired, and they do not write for the overcritical or too shrewd reader.

— FRIEDRICH NIETZSCHE, *Human, All Too Human,* 1880

Every time you turn the page, this guy is masturbating! I think Philip Roth is a good writer, but I wouldn't want to shake hands with him.

— JACQUELINE SUSANN, novelist, quoted in *Lovely Me: The Life of Jacqueline Susann* by Barbara Seaman, 1987

Great writers are not the only interesting writers.

— J. C. SQUIRE, British journalist, in *The London Mercury,* 1933

You can't fake it. Bad writing is a gift.

— RICHARD LE GALLIENNE, English poet and essayist, quoted in *Pieces of Hate* by Heywood Broun, 1922

Good writing is writing that can get published and paid for. If nobody will buy it, then it's not good.

— GARRY PROVOST, "What Writers Should Understand About Money," *1987 Writer's Yearbook*

Writing a book is a horrible, exhausting struggle, like a long bout of some painful illness. One would never undertake such a thing if one were not driven on by some demon whom one can neither resist nor understand.

— GEORGE ORWELL, *Why I Write,* 1953

One not only writes a book. One lives it. Upon completing it there are certain symptoms of death.

    ━ JOHN CHEEVER, novelist, quoted in *Words and Their Masters* by Israel Shenker, 1974

Nothing can destroy the good writer. The only thing that can alter the good writer is death.

    ━ WILLIAM FAULKNER, novelist, quoted in *The Paris Review*, Spring 1956

I have made it appear as though my motives were wholly public-spirited. I don't want to leave that as the final impression. All writers are vain, selfish and lazy, and at the very bottom of their motives lies a mystery.

    ━ GEORGE ORWELL, *Why I Write*, 1953

I write because I like to write.

    ━ PADDY CHAFEVSKY, screenwriter/novelist, quoted in *The Craft of the Screenwriter* by John Brady, 1981

I write to find out.

    ━ Attributed to WILLIAM MANCHESTER, journalist and historian

[Every writer] wants to be loved. He wants people, millions and millions and millions of people to read his book and say, "You are marvelous. I love you."

    ━ EVAN HUNTER, novelist, quoted in *Conversations* by Roy Newquist, 1967

I write for no other purpose than to add to the beauty that now belongs to me. I write a book for no other reason than to add three or four hundred acres to my magnificent estate.

    ━ JACK LONDON, novelist, quoted in *Jack London* by Charles Child Walcutt, 1966

The truth is we write for love. That is why it is so easy to exploit us.

    ━ ERICA JONG, "Doing It for Love," *The Writer*, July 1997

Because I hate. A lot. Hard.

— WILLIAM GASS, novelist, explaining why he writes, quoted in
Why I Write: Thoughts on the Craft of Fiction edited by Will
Blythe, 1998

I do not think that most writers write for money alone. Good ones
write mainly to please themselves and hope at the same time to
please as many other people as possible.

— MERLE MILLER, *Writer's Roundtable*, 1959

Dismissing Dr. Johnson's assertion that "No man but a blockhead
ever wrote except for money," it is safe to say that most writers
aren't in it for the wages, fringe benefits, or short hours. There are
much easier ways to make a buck and few better ways to stay poor.
No. Lurking in the shadows behind every writer is the relentless
spirit of the zealot. The act of writing is an act of faith; someone
will read and perhaps be changed.

— KENNETH C. DAVIS, *Two-Bit Culture*, 1984

Writing is a way of coming to terms with the world and with oneself.

— Attributed to R. V. CASSILL, novelist

The impulse to create beauty is rather rare in literary men . . . Far
ahead of it comes the yearning to make money. And after the yearning to make money comes the yearning to make a noise.

— H. L. MENCKEN, *Prejudices*, 1919

Recognition is everything you write for; it's much more than the
money. You want your books to be valued. It's a basic aspiration of
the serious writer.

— WILLIAM KENNEDY, novelist, quoted in *The New York Times
Magazine*, August 26, 1984

I want to live other lives. I've never quite believed that one chance
is all I get. Writing is my way of making other chances.

— ANNE TYLER, novelist, *Washington Post*, August 15, 1976

It's the closest thing to playing God there is. You can create worlds and destroy them. You can create thousands of characters and manipulate their lives—though sometimes your characters will have a life that goes beyond a pen.

— PAT KUBIS and BOB HOWARD, *Writing Fiction, Nonfiction and How to Publish,* 1985

There are many reasons why novelists write—but they all have one thing in common: a need to create an alternative world.

— JOHN FOWLES, British novelist, quoted in the London *Sunday Times Magazine,* October 2, 1977

I write fiction because I want to escape from what's real and to create something that's completely different.

— ALICE HOFFMAN, novelist, quoted in *The Writer,* November 1994

Writing lets us stay at home. It carries us away from what is unpleasant in everyday life, while at the same time instantly conferring upon us the mythical status of "novelist."

— DONALD MAASS, *The Career Novelist,* 1996

Don't let pretentious literary talk fool you into believing that writers just write for themselves. Writing for yourself alone is creative masturbation. We do write to please ourselves, but basically we write to be read. Writing is not only a means of self-expression and catharsis; it is also a compulsive form of egotistical and infantile exhibitionism.

— IRVING WALLACE, novelist, quoted in *Conversations* by Roy Newquist, 1967

The need to express one's self in writing springs from a maladjustment to life, or from an inner conflict which the adolescent (or the grown man) cannot resolve in action . . . I do not mean that it is enough to be maladjusted to become a great writer, but writing is, for some, a method of resolving a conflict, providing they have the necessary talent.

— ANDRÉ MAUROIS, *The Art of Writing,* 1960

The quality which makes a man want to write and be read is essentially a desire for self-exposure and is masochistic. Like one of those guys who has a compulsion to take his thing out and show it on the street.

━━ JAMES JONES, novelist, quoted in *Writers at Work,* Third Series, 1967

What else is writing but showing off. Writing is the most incredible act of ego anyone can perform.

━━ HARLAN ELLISON, novelist and screenwriter, quoted in *The Complete Guide to Writing Fiction* by Barnaby Conrad, 1990

A person who publishes a book wilfully appears before the public with his pants down.

━━ EDNA ST. VINCENT MILLAY, *Letters,* 1952

Too many people think they can escape from their ailments by becoming writers. I don't object to it as occupational therapy, but writing involves a commitment greater than illness. Writing has to be worked at.

━━ BERNARD MALAMUD, novelist, quoted in *Words and Their Masters* by Israel Shenker, 1974

What motivates a writer to produce a particular work is really nobody's business. Some pretty fair poems have been written because the poet wanted to make time with a young woman, and Balzac did most of his writing because he had no alternative; the creditors were beating on the door, waiting for him to finish so they could get paid.

━━ MERLE MILLER, *Writer's Roundtable,* 1959

There is probably no other trade in which there is so little relationship between profits and actual value, or into which sheer chance so largely enters.

━━ KATHLEEN O'BRIEN, English writer, quoted in *Author! Author!* edited by Richard Findlater, 1984

The money I got for my first novel came out to around $2.50 an hour. I worked on a movie once where the producers wanted the screenplay so fast and so desperately that I made about $500 an hour. It wasn't any better than things I've never been able to sell. Getting paid for writing is a bad joke that has nothing to do with the value of what you've written.

> ⏤JOHN SAYLES, novelist and screenwriter, *The New York Times Book Review,* September 6, 1981

We know our writers can't live on what we're paying them, but we've got a thousand kids out there who'll work for nothing.

> ⏤Unidentified editor in chief of one of the largest mass market circulation magazines, quoted by James Lincoln Collier, "Can Writers Afford to Write Books?" *Publishers Weekly,* July 31, 1981

Of the many people who contribute to the making of a book, from the sweeper at the printing plant, to the publisher in a paneled office, the worst paid, on any basis you care to name is the writer.

> ⏤JAMES LINCOLN COLLIER, "Can Writers Afford to Write Books?" *Publishers Weekly,* July 31, 1981

Of the 250 million people in the United States, maybe sixty or so make a good living from writing fiction.

> ⏤PETER RUBIE, "An Editor Speaks From the Trenches," *The Writer,* September 1992

The annual [financial] report of *New York Review of Books* . . . showed editorial expenses of $44,761 representing fees for contributors— and $102,000 for messengers.

> ⏤MACK CARTER, *Adweek,* February 18, 1985

The book business is the only one I can think of where almost everyone involved is underpaid even though the end user is overcharged.

> ⏤DANIEL AKST, "The Future of the Book," *The Wall Street Journal,* December 18, 1998

Although writing ranks among the top 10 per cent of professions in terms of prestige, writers' incomes prove drastically lower than those of the doctors and lawyers who share the high-esteem rating—and you can't, as the saying goes, eat prestige.

—Jean Strouse, *Newsweek,* June 22, 1981

The vast majority of novelists are still involved in an essentially uneconomical activity.

—James Monaco, *American Film Now,* 1979

Who profits from all this writing activity? The manufacturers of typewriters and typing paper, of course. And the U.S. Post Office.

—William Targ, *Indecent Pleasures,* 1975

A lot of money means a lot of time to write, a real luxury. Time to write is so important that I'm distressed to hear how many people in the literary community seem to frown on commercial success. Of course, the people who frown on it the most actively are those of us who no longer need it; there's at least a little hypocrisy in this.

—Attributed to John Irving, novelist

The only people who claim that money is not important are people who have enough money so that they are relieved of the ugly burden of thinking about it.

—Attributed to Joyce Carol Oates, novelist

There are two tips I would offer beginning writers: 1) Writing for fame or fortune is a fool's errand; 2) Write out of a passion, a caring, a need. The rest will follow.

—Attributed to Sidney Sheldon, novelist

No one can really tell a beginning writer whether or not he has what it takes . . . The young writer must decide for himself, on the available evidence.

—John Gardner, *On Becoming a Novelist,* 1983

If they're meant to be writers, they will write. There's nothing that can stop them.

➤ TENNESSEE WILLIAMS, playwright, quoted in *The Paris Review,*
Fall 1981

A budding free-lance writer should live in New York. After all, it's the seat of most magazine offices—and it's where you meet editors by chance. Most commissions have arisen from casual conversations, and contacts are horribly important. Clearly, kinship with editors cannot really be built through the mails—and certainly not by telephones.

➤ NORA SAYRE, *Mademoiselle,* March 1968

Write what you know. Write what interests you. If you're fascinated, the work will go faster and be more pleasant.

➤ ROBERT W. BLY, *Writer's Digest,* February 1996

If I had to give young writers advice, I'd say don't listen to writers talking about writing.

➤ LILLIAN HELLMAN, playwright, quoted in *The New York Times,*
February 21, 1960

Beware of friends. The only valuable criticism you can get comes from someone who hates you, or at least is trying to tear your work apart.

➤ LAWRENCE TREAT, novelist, quoted in *Writer's Digest,*
September 1986

Keep away from people who try to belittle your ambitions. Small people always do that.

➤ MARK TWAIN, novelist, quoted in *Writer's Digest,* February 1991

It's my experience that very few writers, young or old, are really seeking advice when they give out their work to be read. They want support; they want someone to say, "Good job."

➤ Attributed to JOHN IRVING, novelist

Learn to trust your own judgment, learn inner independence, learn to trust that time will sort good from bad—including your own bad. Do not pay attention to current literary modes, for they can be observed changing, sometimes overnight.

— DORIS LESSING, "Into the Labyrinth," essay in *Author! Author!* edited by Richard Findlater, 1984

The only sound advice I can give to the young writer is to tell him to have faith in himself. Whether he is talented or not, he must have enough faith in himself to disregard all advice and all criticism.

— HOWARD FAST, novelist, quoted in *Counterpoint* compiled and edited by Roy Newquist, 1964

I decided a long time ago that writers should not be encouraged. They should be discouraged. That's more helpful to a writer than encouragement, because I think he's going to learn a lot more that way. If you are going to be a writer, you will be, encouraged or not.

— ERSKINE CALDWELL, novelist, quoted in *The Writer's Digest Guide to Good Writing,* 1994

One should never show an unfinished manuscript to anyone. You are sure to receive opinions contrary to some aspect of what you have written and such opinions, no matter how strong you are, may have a weakening effect upon that conviction you must sustain until your work is done. A book cannot be written by a committee. One must obey oneself alone and take one's chances.

— PAUL HORGAN, *Approaches to Writing,* 1988

The most solid advice to a writer is this, I think. Try to learn and breathe deeply, really to taste food when you eat, and when you sleep, really to sleep. Try as much as possible to be wholly alive, with all your might, and when you laugh, laugh like hell, and when you get angry, get good and angry. Try to be alive. You will be dead soon enough.

— WILLIAM SAROYAN, novelist, quoted in *Contemporary Dramatists* by James Vinson, 1976

The first advice I would give him [the young writer] would be to have him ask himself if he really wants to write, because it's not all that fun.
➤ EVAN HUNTER, novelist, quoted in *Conversations* by Roy Newquist, 1967

Writing is a craft. You have to take your apprenticeship in it like anything else.
➤ KATHERINE ANNE PORTER, novelist and short-story writer, quoted in *The Saturday Review*, March 31, 1962

Nobody becomes Tom Wolfe overnight, not even Tom Wolfe.
➤ WILLIAM ZINSSER, *On Writing Well*, 1976

Melville wasn't ready to write *Moby Dick* until he was five novels into his career.
➤ *The Writer's Digest Handbook of Novel Writing* edited by Tom Clark, 1992

The only way to learn is to force yourself to produce a certain number of words on a regular basis.
➤ WILLIAM ZINSSER, *On Writing Well*, 1976

We are all apprentices in a craft where no one ever becomes a master.
➤ ERNEST HEMINGWAY, novelist, quoted in the *New York Journal-American*, July 11, 1961

There isn't, unfortunately, any way of discovering whether you can write a publishable novel except by writing it.
➤ JOHN BRAINE, *Writing a Novel*, 1974

The young writer would be a fool to follow a theory. Teach yourself by your own mistakes; people learn only by error.
➤ WILLIAM FAULKNER, novelist, quoted in *The Paris Review*, Spring 1956

Tailors and writers must mind the fashion.
➤ THOMAS FULLER, *Gnomologia*, 1732

Always dream and shoot higher than you know how to. Don't bother just to be better than your contemporaries or predecessors. Try to be better than yourself.

— WILLIAM FAULKNER, novelist, quoted in *The Paris Review,*
   Spring 1956

When I write, I aim in my mind not toward New York but toward a vague spot a little to the east of Kansas. I think of the books on library shelves, without their jackets, years old, and a countryish teen-aged boy finding them, and having them speak to him. The reviewers, the stacks in Brentanos, are just hurdles to get over, to place the books on that shelf.

— JOHN UPDIKE, novelist, quoted in *Writers at Work,* Fourth Series,
   1976

The chief reason that so many of the great classics seem to speak so directly to us is that the authors were consciously trying to reach us, or at least people with an astonishing resemblance to us.

— MASON W. GROSS, former president, Rutgers College, speech,
   National Book Committee, November 18, 1959, reprinted in *Writing in America* edited by John Fischer and Robert B. Silvers, 1960

For those who say the paperback original is designed to appeal to the masses, let it be pointed out that Shakespeare, too, appealed to the masses. He wrote within a formula that demanded action and sword play, puns and low humor, and noblemen and noblewomen as heroes and heroines.

— LAWRENCE TREAT, *Mystery Writer's Handbook,* 1976

He writes nothing whose readings are not read.

— MARTIAL, *Epigrams from Martial: A Verse Translation* by Barriss
   Mills, 1969

Every act of communication presupposes a communicator and an audience . . . It's kind of a social contract. One doesn't pay $10.00 for a book in order to be bored.

— MORRIS WEST, "How to Write a Novel," *The Writer,* May 1977

It is the writer's fault, not the reader's, if the reader puts down the book.

➤ Attributed to DAVID HALBERSTAM, author

The best book is a collaboration between author and reader.

➤ BARBARA TUCHMAN, *Practicing History*, 1981

I have found that sometimes it helps to pick out one person—a real person you know, or an imagined person, and write to that one.

➤ JOHN STEINBECK, letter to Robert Wallsten, February 13–14, 1962, reprinted in *Steinbeck: A Life in Letters* edited by Elaine Steinbeck and Robert Wallsten, 1975

An author ought to write for the youth of his own generation, the critics of the next, and schoolmasters of ever after.

➤ F. SCOTT FITZGERALD, novelist, quoted in *The Guardian*, November 13, 1964

The desire for the greatest number of readers is to me not only justifiable, but a proper ambition for every writer to entertain.

➤ W. B. MAXWELL, English writer, quoted in *Author! Author!* edited by Richard Findlater, 1984

If someone deliberately sets out to write a best seller, what he is really saying is that he is going to write a book that will appeal to everyone. In essence, what he is looking for is the lowest common denominator. I believe when you try to appeal to everyone, the result is that you end up appealing to almost no one. Every good writer that I know writes to please himself, not to please others.

➤ SIDNEY SHELDON, "The Magical World of the Novelist," *The Writer*, November 1980

Our American professors like their literature clear and cold and pure and very dead.

➤ SINCLAIR LEWIS, novelist, speech to the Swedish Academy accepting the Nobel Prize for Literature, December 12, 1930, quoted in *Literature 1901–67* by Horst Frenz, 1969

There is no formula which may be depended upon to produce a bestseller. There are too many impalpable considerations, too many chances and accidents, too complex a combination of conditions affecting the writing, publication, and selling of a book that make the attainment of the top rank by even the most promising candidate a certainty.

— FRANK LUTHER MOTT, *Golden Multitudes: The Story of Bestsellers in the United States,* 1947

The proof that no such formula exists is the extremely small number of best-sellers in relation to the total number of novels published.

— JOHN BRAINE, *Writing a Novel,* 1974

Writers who concentrate on pleasing all the time don't have much ultimate impact. One of the functions of an author is to arouse.

— Attributed to WILLIAM STYRON, novelist

I don't want to be studied in English classes; I want to be read.

— TIM O'BRIEN, novelist, quoted in *The New York Times Book Review,* June 8, 1980

Index

Leonard, John, 19, 157
Lesher, Stephen, 62
Lessing, Doris, 21, 144, 169
Levant, Oscar, 78
Levine, Ellen, 39
Levine, Faye, 35, 125
Lewis, Charles, 49
Lewis, F. R., 81
Lewis, Joseph, 8
Lewis, Sinclair, 55, 75, 172
Limerick, Patricia Nelson, 115
Lippman, Jeff, 90
Litowinsky, Olga, 22
London, Jack, 162
Long, John, 14, 118
Longfellow, Henry Wadsworth, 17
Love, Nancy, 37
Lowell, James Russell, 45
Lowell, Robert, 17, 80
Lund, Peter, 9, 103
Lynch, Frederick R., 98
Lynes, Russell, 66
Lyttle, Mark Hamilton, 29

Maass, Donald, 95, 164
MacCampbell, Donald, 23, 40, 92
MacLeod, Iaian, 32
Madden, David, 71
Mailer, Norman, 13, 15, 55, 144, 156
Malamud, Bernard, 118, 120, 121, 165
Malcolm, Janet, 2, 64
Manchester, William, 33, 162

Mann, Thomas, 8
Marek, Richard, 93, 134
Margolin, Phillip W., 157
Margolis, Jon, 62
Marple, Allen, 150
Marquis, Donald, 80, 151
Martial, 171
Martin, Paul Raymond, 71
Marx, Groucho, 46
Marx, Karl, 32
Maugham, W. Somerset, 76, 148, 151
Maurois, Andre, 20, 164
Maxwell, W. B., 172
Mayes, Herbert R., 110
McCarthy, Desmond, 3
McConnell, Malcolm, 71
McCullough, Colleen, 22
McDowell, Edwin, 36, 118
McFarland, Thomas, 103
McGrady, Mike, 35
McGuane, Thomas, 129
McInerney, Jay, 156
McLaughlin, Mignon, 157
McNeil, William, 31
McPherson, William, 27
McTiernan, John, 127
McWilliams, Peter A., 77, 134
Melville, Herman, 57
Mencken, H. L., 61, 163
Metalius, Grace, 145
Michener, James, 69, 132, 142, 152, 158
Mill, John Stuart, 8
Millay, Edna St. Vincent, 165
Miller, Merle, 163, 165

About the Author

William A. Gordon is a full-time author and publisher. He has also written *The Ultimate Hollywood Tour Book; Shot on This Site: A Traveler's Guide to the Places and Locations Used to Film Famous Movies and Television Shows;* and *Four Dead in Ohio: Was There a Conspiracy at Kent State?* He lives in Southern California.